Five directors

Manchester University Press

FRENCH FILM DIRECTORS

DIANA HOLMES and ROBERT INGRAM *series editors*
DUDLEY ANDREW *series consultant*

Jean-Jacques Beineix PHIL POWRIE
Luc Besson SUSAN HAYWARD
Bertrand Blier SUE HARRIS
Robert Bresson KEITH READER
Leos Carax GARIN DOWD AND FERGUS DALEY
Claude Chabrol GUY AUSTIN
Henri-Georges Clouzot CHRISTOPHER LLOYD
Jean Cocteau JAMES WILLIAMS
Claire Denis MARTINE BEUGNET
Marguerite Duras RENATE GÜNTHER
Georges Franju KATE INCE
Jean-Luc Godard DOUGLAS MORREY
Mathieu Kassovitz WILL HIGBEE
Diane Kurys CARRIE TARR
Patrice Leconte LISA DOWNING
Louis Malle HUGO FREY
Georges Méliès ELIZABETH EZRA
Maurice Pialat MARJA WAREHIME
Jean Renoir MARTIN O'SHAUGHNESSY
Alain Resnais EMMA WILSON
Eric Rohmer DEREK SCHILLING
Coline Serreau BRIGITTE ROLLET
André Téchiné BILL MARSHALL
François Truffaut DIANA HOLMES AND ROBERT INGRAM
Agnès Varda ALISON SMITH
Jean Vigo MICHAEL TEMPLE

Five directors
Auteurism from Assayas to Ozon

EDITED BY KATE INCE

Manchester University Press
MANCHESTER AND NEW YORK

distributed exclusively in the USA by Palgrave

Published by Manchester University Press
Oxford Road, Manchester M13 9NR, UK
and Room 400, 175 Fifth Avenue, New York, NY 10010, USA
www.manchesteruniversitypress.co.uk

Distributed exclusively in the USA by
Palgrave, 175 Fifth Avenue, New York, NY 10010, USA

Distributed exclusively in Canada by
UBC Press, University of British Columbia, 2029 West Mall, Vancouver, BC, Canada V6T 1Z2

British Library Cataloguing-in-Publication Data
A catalogue record for this book is available from the British Library

Library of Congress Cataloging-in-Publication Data applied for

ISBN 978 07190 7431 8 *hardback*

First published 2008

17 16 15 14 13 12 11 10 09 08   10 9 8 7 6 5 4 3 2 1

Typeset in Scala with Meta display
by Koinonia, Manchester
Printed in Great Britain
by MPG Books Ltd, Bodmin, Cornwall

Contents

Series editors' foreword

To an anglophone audience, the combination of the words 'French' and 'cinema' evokes a particular kind of film: elegant and wordy, sexy but serious – an image as dependent upon national stereotypes as is that of the crudely commercial Hollywood blockbuster, which is not to say that either image is without foundation. Over the past two decades, this generalised sense of a significant relationship between French identity and film has been explored in scholarly books and articles, and has entered the curriculum at university level and, in Britain, at A-level. The study of film as art-form and (to a lesser extent) as industry, has become a popular and widespread element of French Studies, and French cinema has acquired an important place within Film Studies. Meanwhile, the growth in multi-screen and 'art-house' cinemas, together with the development of the video industry, has led to the greater availability of foreign-language films to an English-speaking audience. Responding to these developments, this series is designed for students and teachers seeking information and accessible but rigorous critical study of French cinema, and for the enthusiastic filmgoer who wants to know more.

The adoption of a director-based approach raises questions about auteurism. A series that categorises films not according to period or to genre (for example), but to the person who directed them, runs the risk of espousing a romantic view of film as the product of solitary inspiration. On this model, the critic's role might seem to be that of discovering continuities, revealing a necessarily coherent set of themes and motifs which correspond to the particular genius of the individual. This is not our aim: the auteur perspective on film, itself most clearly articulated in France in the early 1950s, will be interrogated in certain volumes of the series, and, throughout, the director will be treated as one highly significant element in a complex process of film production and reception which includes socio-economic and political determinants, the work of a large and highly skilled team of artists and technicians, the mechanisms of production and distribution, and the complex and multiply determined responses of spectators.

The work of some of the directors in the series is already well known outside France, that of others is less so – the aim is both to provide informative and original English-language studies of established figures, and to extend the range of French directors known to anglophone students of cinema. We intend the series to contribute to the promotion of the formal and informal study of French films, and to the pleasure of those who watch them.

DIANA HOLMES
ROBERT INGRAM

Acknowledgements

I would like to express my gratitude to Diana Holmes and Robert Ingram for their initial interest in this project, and to the anonymous readers who helped shape it into a volume that could not properly have contained the word 'French' in its title, despite consisting of essays on filmmakers working in the French language. My thanks go also to Matthew Frost at Manchester University Press for his ready professional advice, and to my contributors, who have been a pleasure to work with.

Introduction

Kate Ince

Auteur cinema in the twentieth century

It is a commonplace to associate *auteur* cinema with France, but for a good reason: as everyone knows, it was a Frenchman, François Truffaut, who launched the polemic that grew into the body of criticism we now know as '*auteur* theory'. However, some directors did enjoy an identity very like what we now understand as a cinematic author before the French *politique des auteurs* began in the early to mid-1950s: René Prédal identifies Georges Méliès as the first *auteur* because he was the

> concepteur unique, seul maître d'ouvrage tout au long de la chaîne de fabrication, mais auteur aussi au sens de créateur d'un univers personnel et imaginaire sans aucune référence réaliste'. (Prédal 2001: 10)[1]

At the same time as taking the origins of auteurism back to the 1900s, however, Prédal makes the necessary and important qualification that the term *auteur* would never have been used of an artist such as Méliès so early in film history: the first filmmakers were known, in French, as *cinémateur* or *écraniste* when the writer or speaker wanted to draw attention to the novelty of cinema as a medium and a technology, as *metteur en scène* when s/he wished to stress the proximity of film directing to directing in the theatre, or as *réalisateur* when a consensual term was required that referred to no specific art form and carried

---

1 'sole conceiver and controller of the work right along the production line, [and] ...in the sense that he was the creator of a personal and imaginary universe entirely lacking in realistic reference'.

with it no historical 'baggage' (Prédal 2001: 10). An additional important term highlighted by Prédal is *cinéaste* – important because it was
not interchangeable with the other words employed, but implied a
judgement of particular value, and was reserved, at least by the critic
Louis Delluc, for 'ceux ... *qui ont fait quelque chose pour l'industrie artis-
tique du cinéma*' (Prédal 2001: 11, original emphasis).[2] Prédal extends
his review of the various names used to designate the creators of
films to English, listing 'filmmaker', 'author' (of a script), 'producer'
and 'director' as the alternatives in circulation before the *politique des
auteurs*, since when – a point he as a French critic understandably
does not make – the French word for authoring has been adopted
by anglophone critics and become the standard film-critical term
for the activity. Another Frenchman commenting on debates about
auteurism, the director-turned-critic Jean-Charles Tacchella, insists
rather more than Prédal on the French status of 'origin' or 'creator'
of the film designated by the concept of the *auteur*, but affirms at
the same time that this primacy of the director 'en tant que principal
artisan, animateur et meneur de jeu d'un film' asserted itself first
'aux Etats-Unis en 1914 et, en France, trois ans plus tard' (Jeancolas,
Meusy and Pinel 1996: 11).[3] In the US, though, the rocketing fame and
power of directors such as Griffith, Chaplin and DeMille so alarmed
Hollywood's producers that they united to reassert control over the
industry, a control they were never again to relinquish. According to
Tacchella, only one director in 1920s America argued the directorial
point of view against this producers' putsch, and this was an émigré
Frenchman, Maurice Tourneur, whose open letter to American
producers exclaimed

> Vous ne pouvez pas dire à un artiste peintre ce qu'il doit peindre, ni
> quelles couleurs il doit employer, ni de quelle dimension doit être la
> toile – et espérer attendre de lui un chef-d'oeuvre![4]

2 'all those ... *who have done something for the artistic industry of the cinema*'. Steven
  Bernas points out that the Dictionnaire Robert dates *cinéaste* to 1920 (Bernas
  2002: 23), and goes on to make very similar points to Prédal about terminology
  (Bernas 2002: 137).
3 'as principal artisan, organiser and leader of a film', 'in the United States in 1914,
  and in France three years later'.
4 'You simply cannot tell a painter what he should paint, what colours he should
  use, and what size the canvas should be – and expect him to produce a masterpiece!'. Tourneur's letter was published in *Variety* on 28 June 1923 (Jeancolas,
  Meusy and Pinel 1996: 12).

Tourneur returned to France three years after this letter was published, having given up the fight to maintain artistic control over 'his' films (Jeancolas, Meusy and Pinel 1996: 12).

The pre-history of auteurism I have introduced above draws solely on recent French critical sources. As I shall go on to show, there have been vigorous debates about the condition and prospects of *auteur* cinema in France over the last decade, debates that seem mostly to have gone unreported in anglophone criticism of francophone cinema. But these have been paralleled by a revival of international debate about the status of the *auteur*: in their extended chapter on *auteur* cinema added to the second edition of Cook's *The Cinema Book* (1999), Pam Cook and Mieke Bernink observe that this was definitely underway by 1995. In 1993 Dudley Andrew had written, 'After a dozen years of clandestine whispering we are permitted to mention, even to discuss, the *auteur* again' (Andrew 1993: 77), and in 1995 the journals *Film History* and *Film Criticism* both published special issues on auteurism. In 2003, two anthologies of essays appeared whose editorial introductions review the history of the concept of the *auteur* and relate it to contemporary developments in the global film industry, called (with a symmetry that suggests their authors were aware of putting together complementary or rival publications) *Authorship and Film* and *Film and Authorship* respectively. While the two editors of *Authorship and Film* specify that the essays in their book 'provide methodological exemplars for poststructuralist authorship study' (Gerstner and Steiger 2003: xi–xii), and write two complementary introductions that focus particularly (and sometimes tortuously, in my view) on the issue of agency, Virginia Wright Wexman's introduction to *Film and Authorship* confines itself to more familiar critical history. As a bridge to my discussion of recent debates about the *auteur* in France, I shall now summarise the development of auteurism as a field up to the 1990s, drawing particularly on Wright Wexman's historical overview.

According to Wright Wexman, the term *auteur* was first used to refer to a film director by Jean Epstein in 1921: her reason for making this point, however, is not to upstage the centrality of Truffaut and other critics at *Cahiers du cinéma* in inaugurating the *politique des auteurs* in the 1950s, but simply to emphasise that 'historically, the most influential work on film authors has taken place in the pages of select journals and cultural institutions in France, England and the United States' (Wright Wexman 2003: 2). Attacking the Tradition of Quality they saw as dominating French post-war film production, Truffaut and his fellow critics instead championed 'moviemakers who managed to produce visually distinctive films under the constraints of the Hollywood studio system' (Wright Wexman 2003: 2–3). Their policy (*politique*) of looking at films in terms of authors was highly political (*une politique* can also be translated as 'a politics'), since it encouraged critics to master the entire body of a director's output in order to discern privileged moments of personal vision detectable in a film's *mise en scène*. Directors picked out for the *auteur* treatment, which comprised reverential praise and extended interviews intended to increase the recipients' stature, included Samuel Fuller, Nicholas Ray, Vincent Minnelli, Douglas Sirk and Alfred Hitchcock from Hollywood, as well as European filmmakers like Max Ophuls, Robert Bresson and Roberto Rossellini.

After Truffaut, Jean-Luc Godard, Eric Rohmer and their colleagues at *Cahiers* turned from criticism to directing in the late 1950s, the 'Romantic auteurist' ideology spawned by the *politique des auteurs* was taken to America by Andrew Sarris, who had spent 1962 in Paris, encountered the *nouvelle vague*, and acted as editor of the English language version of *Cahiers du cinéma*, as well as writing for influential American magazines such as *Film Culture* and *The Village Voice*. In Sarris's hands, however, the *auteur* theory (as it became known in English) turned into a means of ranking directors in order of merit: his 1968 book *The American Cinema* famously consisted of a pantheon of two hundred filmmakers that gave pride of place to Hollywood's own. The 1960s in England, meanwhile, saw the formation of another group of auteurists (Robin Wood, Ian Cameron, Victor Perkins) around the journal *Movie*, founded in 1962. Although their writings were steeped in the climate of auteurism that reigned in the early 1960s and included many interviews with filmmakers, the *Movie* critics were influenced as much by the New Criticism then dominating the field of literature as they were by *Cahiers du cinéma*, and are distinguishable from the *politique des auteurs* by their tolerance and even embracing of literariness, a tendency often detectable in their close readings of individual films.

Following the advent of structuralism and structuralist approaches to narrative and communication in the mid 1960s, a type of auteurism was born that preserved a focus on authorship at the very moment when Roland Barthes was polemically declaring the author dead, in his famous essay 'The death of the author'. This was *auteur*-structuralism, an approach which 'identified the style of a given director with a series of structuring oppositions that recurred throughout his or her oeuvre' (Wright Wexman 2003: 4–5). *Auteur*-structuralism was forged in the British Film Institute's Educational Division and best represented in work by Geoffrey Nowell-Smith and Peter Wollen, on Visconti and John Ford respectively. Meanwhile at *Cahiers du cinéma*, a new editorial regime that was both more intellectual and more political than the 'jeunes Turcs' of the *nouvelle vague* did not abandon auteurism completely, despite declaring, in 1965, that the *politique des auteurs* was officially over. Jean-Louis Comolli and Jean Narboni's 1969 essay 'Cinema/Ideology/Criticism' created a series of categories into which all films could be placed, and put particular emphasis on category 'E': although analyses of category 'E' films located the formal subversion attributed to these films in their discourse (*discours*) rather than in any agent or psychological entity outside the text, it was apparent to anyone looking at the list of these films' directors that category 'E' had become a sort of new name for *auteur* cinema. The famous *Cahiers* collective essay on John Ford's *Young Mr. Lincoln* (one such category 'E' film) was matched by work by Raymond Bellour on Hitchcock which, although it analysed the director's place in his film-texts in terms of 'enunciative presence', was undeniably of an auteurist strain. *Cahiers*' new theoretico-political agenda from the late 1960s on focused on Althusser's Lacanian-influenced work on ideology and on the spectator of the film as a producer of meaning (Barthes' 'The death of the author' essay ends by championing the reader), and as Wright Wexman points out, was energetically adopted

> as the program of *Screen*, a journal sponsored in part by the British Film Institute and edited by a group that included Ben Brewster, Ed Buscombe, Pam Cook, Christine Gledhill, Stephen Heath, Claire Johnston, Colin MacCabe, Laura Mulvey, Geoffrey Nowell-Smith, Sam Rohdie, Paul Willemen, and Peter Wollen ... At the same time, *Screen* perpetuated the auteurist tradition by publishing interviews with directors like Douglas Sirk and Pier Paolo Pasolini as well as special issues on Jean-Marie Straub, Nagisa Oshima, and Jean-Luc Godard. (Wright Wexman 2003: 6–7)

Through the heyday of what came to be known as 'screen theory', and after the rise to prominence of the poststructuralist philosophies of Derrida, Foucault, Lyotard and others in the 1970s, thinking about the *auteur* shifted towards the film-text as the place where meaning was produced. The authorship of films did not become irrelevant, but was conceptualised as a product of the textual system and of the reception of films by spectators, rather than as a source or origin of meaning. The *auteur* became just one of the organising principles of coherence in film, with more critical attention going to genre(s) and stars as alternative paradigms. From around 1980 onwards, as Dudley Andrew's 1993 remark about 'a dozen years of clandestine whispering' quoted above indicates, *auteur* theory effectively went underground: highly individual directors of course continued to direct, and film critics continued to study and write about them, but the *auteur* ceased to be a focus of critical attention and debate. Until the early 1990s, that is, when a clutch of significant articles about auteurism appeared once again: Andrew's 'The unauthorized auteur today', James Naremore's 'Authorship and the cultural politics of film criticism', and Timothy Corrigan's *A Cinema Without Walls* (1991), the first book to recognise and explore how auteurism had become an important commercial strategy in late twentieth-century cinema.

Auteurism in France 1995–2005

Following Timothy Corrigan, Phil Powrie recognises that the notion of the *auteur* has been 'one of the most successful of French cinema's marketing strategies' (Powrie 1999: 8), and he also points out that attempts were made during the 1980s to 'reinvigorate' the notion of the *auteur* 'by an emphasis on "art cinema"' in a very literal sense: films which dwelt on painting (e.g. Godard's *Passion*, 1982; Cavalier's *Thérèse*, 1986), coupled with a sustained attempt by the *Cahiers du cinéma* to valorize auteurism through the academic link between cinema and painting' (Powrie 1999: 8). A further significant boost to the re-emergence of auteurism as a significant force was the establishment of the Franco-German television station Arte, with its cinephilic agenda, in the early 1990s (Powrie 1999: 8–9; Prédal 2002: 54–5). But 1995 was of course the centenary of the birth of cinema, and in France as elsewhere the commissioning of a first critical history of the *auteur* was an obvious way to mark the occasion. The co-authored volume by Jean-Pierre Jeancolas, Jean-Jacques Meusy and Vincent Pinel that resulted, *L'Auteur du film*, is subtitled *Description d'un combat*, and one of the first things Jeancolas underlines is that 'le statut de l'auteur est au coeur du conflit commercial qui a dressé face à face les Européens et les Américains dans les années quatre-vingt dix' (Jeancolas, Meusy and Pinel 1996: 120).[5] Something of a new war of words seems to have been engaged between books, the pages of *Cahiers du cinéma* and national newspapers such as *Le Monde* and *Libération* in the years following 1995, starting with Antoine de Baecque's article 'Aux aguets: que reste-t-il de la politique des auteurs?' in 1997, continuing with René Prédal's *Le Cinéma d'auteur, une vieille lune?* in 2001, and culminating (perhaps) in the weighty tome devoted to the subject by Steven Bernas in 2002. Much of the history of the status of the *auteur* specific to post-war France has to be extricated from the enduring struggles for legislation aiming to afford better protection for directors concerned to assert moral ownership of their films through the concept of the *droit d'auteur*, a combat which has in many ways served as an example to other European countries seeking to emulate or benefit from the productivity of France's film culture. In this section I shall summarise the legal advances achieved by these struggles, and in the next, having considered the directors featured in this book, assess how *auteur* cinema is still, some years into the twenty-first century, one vital pole of francophone film production – albeit in a very different form from that envisaged by the *politique des auteurs* in the 1950s.

An official status was first accorded to directors of French films, as distinct from the authors of other cultural forms, by the law of 11 March 1957. A commission on intellectual property presided over by Professor Jean Escarra (usually known as the 'commission Escarra') had been assembling this legislation since the Liberation of Paris in August 1944, and finally turned it over to parliament in June 1954 (Jeancolas, Meusy and Pinel 1996: 146). In article 14, which related specifically to cinema, the director (*réalisateur*) of a film was for the first time granted co-authorship of the work along with the scriptwriter, the author of any adaptation, the author of any spoken commentary, and the composer of the film's music (Jeancolas, Meusy and Pinel 1996: 148). For some, this recognition of a film as an essentially collaborative work, authored by up to five different people, was contradicted by a clause in the law that granted the right of disclosure (*droit de divulgation*) to only the director and the producer, and

5 'the status of the *auteur* is at the heart of the commercial conflict that produced the stand-off between Europeans and Americans in the 1990s'.

for others the new law did not go far enough (Jeancolas, Meusy and Pinel 1996: 153). After it took effect early in 1958, however, the Société des auteurs et compositeurs dramatiques (SACD), the established body that had protected the interests of film directors thus far, created a special service internal to its organisation to deal with all their business affairs, such as the drafting and management of contracts between a film's director-author and its producer. Although it was not an independent body, the SACD's 'service cinéma' was the first in a number of new organisations that would serve film *auteurs* working in France in the second half of the twentieth century. Principal among these were the Société des réalisateurs de films (SRF) and Auteurs-réalisateurs-producteurs, or L'ARP. The first of these was born out of the events of May 1968, and held its first meeting at the premises of the French Cinémathèque on 25 June of that year, presided over by Robert Bresson (Jeancolas, Meusy and Pinel 1996: 155). The SRF quickly became a pressure group that would exert considerable influence for over three decades, for instance by creating the Cannes film festival's *Quinzaine des réalisateurs* in 1969 (Jeancolas, Meusy and Pinel 1996: 159). In 1988 both the SRF and the SACD were involved in the legal action brought against the French television station La Cinq by the rightsholders of John Huston's film *The Asphalt Jungle* (1950), for preparing to broadcast a version of the film colourised by Ted Turner's media corporation. In December 1994 the court of Versailles ruled conclusively that to colourise an audiovisual work against the will of its creator was to infringe his or her moral ownership of that work, and that French law held sway in France even when the author in question was not a French national (Jeancolas, Meusy and Pinel 1996: 160).

L'ARP, the second pressure group that would be so influential in winning the 'exception culturelle' on European audiovisual products in the 1993 GATT talks, was formed on the initiative of Claude Berri in 1987, and remained distinct from the SRF by concerning itself with the material rather than the legal issues in which film directors needed protection (Jeancolas, Meusy and Pinel 1996: 165). Before this, however, in 1985, the second major law on film authorship had been passed, having been prepared during Jack Lang's decisive period as François Mitterand's first Minister of Culture. In spite of vigorous last-minute opposition by a group of producers, who argued that *auteurs* were already better protected in France than anywhere else in the world, the 1985 law granted the status of 'auteur privilégié' to directors, a notable advance on the co-authorship legislated on in 1957. The new status meant that the definitive version of a film was decided by agreement between the director (or joint directors) and the producer, with any modification to this version representing an infringement of the director's moral right to ownership of his or her film (Jeancolas, Meusy and Pinel 1996: 163–4).

Retracing, albeit summarily, these campaigns for the rights of directors carefully documented by Jean-Pierre Jeancolas in *L'Auteur du film*, provides the background to the debate about the role of the *auteur* in French film culture that has taken place since 1995. As I intimated above, Antoine de Baecque may perhaps be held responsible for initiating this, since he ended his 1997 article 'Aux aguets: que reste-t-il de la politique des auteurs?' with the suggestion that auteurism be abandoned altogether as a critical paradigm. Earlier in the article, De Baecque makes the important point that film criticism often now tends simply to identify films as signs of their directors, for which he coins the useful term 'auteurification', a *politique des auteurs* become dogma, in which the personalities of the favoured directors become myths (De Baecque 1997: 22). But although his view that film criticism has more important things to do than make collections of *auteurs* (De Baecque 1997: 23) invites sympathy, De Baecque's suggested alternative – that films be seen not as markers in the identifiable 'brand' of a director's career but as 'des apparitions éclatées dessinant un paysage cinématographique changeant et éphémère' (De Baecque 1997: 24)[6] – reveals him evasively and timorously skirting round the entire issue of auteurism, with its undeniable place in French and international film history, and its possible continuing relevance in a globalised film culture. The 'éloge de la divagation' he calls for at the end of his article is glib, a weak and unsatisfactory argument. In *L'Auteur au cinéma*, Steven Bernas attacks it for these and other reasons, commenting that 'Refouler un mot dans le néant, c'est gagner la guerre des illusions. C'est rêver un pouvoir symbolique sur le réel' (Bernas 2002: 252).[7]

The debate set in train by De Baecque's article was not confined to the pages of film journals: a much less qualified attack by Noël Burch

---

6 'fragmented appearances that outline a changing and fleeting cinematographic landscape'.

7 'eulogy to [discursive] rambling'. 'To abolish a word entirely is to win an illusory war. It's a fantasy of symbolic power over the real'.

entitled simply 'Contre l'auteurisme' appeared in the daily newspaper *Libération* on 5 August 1998. This was countered in turn by René Prédal in *Le Cinéma d'auteur, une vieille lune?* who argues convincingly that Burch's attack, carried out 'au nom d'un cinéma populaire qui racontait des histoires et savait procurer au public un véritable plaisir',[8] simplistically identifies *auteur* cinema with modernism and formalism, themselves complex movements he reduces to simple formulae for the purposes of his polemic (Prédal 2001: 132). Prédal himself pragmatically recognises that auteurism can only be given a plural definition and will continue to shift in meaning, even as *auteur* films remain a significant part of francophone film culture:

> Matérialisation aussi bien cinéphilique que professionnelle et commerciale de la notion d'auteur, le cinéma d'auteur existe ... Successivement refusé, toléré, victorieux et contesté, il est également fragile, changeant et pluriel, sujet à des exclusions ou des récuperations comme à des définitions et des exégèses divergentes. (Prédal 2001: 136–7)[9]

One dimension of this plurality of *auteur* cinema specific to the 1990s, and widely commented on by both the French critical establishment and in the anglophone world, is the auteurist tendency of the *jeune cinéma français*. The very existence of a movement constituting a *jeune cinéma français* during the 1990s has been contested by voices as authoritative as Jean-Pierre Jeancolas (Jeancolas 2005), and I shall not enter into that debate here: as Ginette Vincendeau says:

> The question of a 'young' French cinema has been on the critical agenda ever since the new wave introduced youth as a supreme factor in cinematic innovation. Since the 1960s critics of French cinema have been keen to find successors to the original new wave, and various 'new new waves' have been detected. (Vincendeau 2005: 33)

Vincendeau goes on to say, however, that the expression *jeune cinéma français* did seem 'genuinely justified' (Vincendeau 2005: 33) in the 1990s by the fact that over one third of the decade's production was

8 'in the name of a popular cinema that told stories and really knew how to entertain the public'.

9 '*Auteur* cinema exists, as a cinephile as well as a professional and a commercial manifestation of the notion of the *auteur* ... In its time it has been rejected, tolerated, victorious and contested, and it remains fragile, shifting and plural, getting repeatedly excluded and recuperated as well as defined and interpreted in various ways'.

made by new filmmakers, and, in order to simplify the enormous diversity of the hundreds of films involved, divides the *jeune cinéma français* into 'two major trends', one of which she calls the 'French *auteurs*' trend (the other is a 'genre-oriented – and more masculine – cinema' associated with a group of male directors) (Vincendeau 2005: 34). She associates the 'French *auteurs*' trend with directors such as Xavier Beauvois, Arnaud Desplechin, Sandrine Veysset, Laetitia Masson and Bruno Dumont, and describes it as a cinema of '"small" *auteur* films appealing to a select cinephile audience, financed predominantly with the help of the *avance sur recettes* and often the Arte channel' (Vincendeau 2005: 34). However restricted or comprehensive a definition one attempts to give to the *jeune cinéma français* (if one attempts to define it at all), the relative youth of the directors of films of personal expression made in French in the 1990s and 2000s is undoubtedly a significant factor in the continuing health of *auteur* cinema in recent years.[10]

Assayas to Ozon: the *auteurs*

The context of the careers and filmographies of three of the directors in this book – Olivier Assayas, Jacques Audiard and François Ozon – is the cinema of France. All Audiard's feature films have been funded entirely by French production companies, and this is also true of the majority of Assayas's output, the main exceptions being his *Cinéaste de notre temps: HHH, portrait de Hou Hsiao Hsien* (1997), to which Taiwanese and Chinese companies contributed, and *Clean* (2004), which has British co-production credits. Despite the wide international distribution of Ozon's films, all his features have been backed by French Fidelité Productions, and increasingly by the cinematic arms of French television companies, such as France 2 Cinéma. Where the Belgian Dardenne brothers (to whom I shall refer as one director, given the near-interchangeability of the directing and producing roles of Jean-Pierre and Luc Dardenne on their four features to date) and Michael Haneke are concerned, however, the picture is more complex, and probably more indicative of current trends in francophone cinema.

All four of the Dardenne brothers' features have been set in

10 For a detailed discussion, see e.g. Prédal 2002, Chapter 3.

Seraing, the town in eastern Belgium in which they are based, whose bleak post-industrial landscape stands in for many similar-looking locations across northern Europe, and is hugely suggestive of the fragile social bonds now characterising the communities that inhabit such places. Although Les Films du Fleuve and other Belgian companies have backed all the brothers' features, their last two features *Le Fils* (2002) and *L'Enfant* (2005) both received support from French producers Archipel, with *L'Enfant* also getting backing from the CNC, Canal Plus, Arte France Cinéma, and the European Community's Eurimages fund. On account of the funding, setting and thematics of their films, then, the Dardenne brothers straddle a position across Belgian and French 'nation-state' cinemas (Crofts 1998) that blurs the distinction between the two. Haneke's account of the making of his first French-language film, *Code inconnu* (2000), makes it clear that another city than Paris could have stood in for the multicultural capital whose socially disconnected population he wanted to feature, and *La Pianiste* (2001), his second film in French, falls into an arguably artificial category of 'European' films in which language inexplicably fails to correspond with setting (it takes place in Vienna). With his most recent film *Caché* (2005) Haneke seems to focus on more specifically French historical traumas, but his third feature *Le Temps du loup* (2003), like *Code inconnu*, thematises intercultural dynamics and trajectories that might relate to many a European nation. Although all Haneke's francophone films have received majority French funding, they have also had Austrian, Romanian, German and Italian financial support. More telling where his status as a European '*auteur*' is concerned is the identity of the producer who brought him into French-language filmmaking, Marin Karmitz, the owner of France's MK2 chain of cinemas, who is renowned for his inclination to back films that do not obviously belong in the twenty-first century multiplex. As Olivier Joyard points out in an article about how a new class of international 'superauteurs' (Hou Hsiao Hsien, Wong Kar-wai, Abbas Kiarostami) have recently worked with French producers, it is – contrary to a widely held belief – more because of these producers' cinephile tendencies and active soliciting of talent than because of the CNC and structures of public funding that internationally renowned directors are often now drawn into the French film industry and its culture.[11]

11 Olivier Joyard, 'Auteurs, classe affaires', *Cahiers du cinéma* 568 (May 2002), 82–3.

Karmitz has produced just Haneke's *Code inconnu* and *La Pianiste* to date, but Haneke's auteurist credentials have been maintained in his subsequent association with Les Films du Losange, the company originally established by Eric Rohmer and Barbet Schroder in 1962, the highpoint of creativity of the *nouvelle vague*.

A consideration of the five directors featured in this book, then, suggests that although France is maintaining its traditional strength as a base for *auteurs* who can reasonably be placed squarely within the national frame, it is also seeing a notable loosening of the borders of its film industry, and developing artistic and financial links that are fully embroiled in the dynamics of globalisation and stretch well beyond its European neighbours. Having noted the rapidly changing film-industrial climate in which the films of Assayas, Audiard, the Dardenne brothers, Haneke and Ozon find themselves, however, it is important to return to the focus of this volume, auteurism, and look at how the phenomenon referred to by the term has developed since Truffaut, Godard *et al.* made it a critical watchword fifty years ago. What changes to the nature of *auteur* cinema are demonstrated by the films of these five directors, and what do the changes tell us about the current condition of francophone cinema?

One theme common to the films of Audiard, the Dardenne brothers, Haneke and Ozon is the perceptible disintegration of the nuclear, heterosexual family. In Ozon's films, the patriarchal family is the main site of drama, comedy, fantasy and subversion, but the other three directors also draw attention to the fragility and loosening of the bonds that underpin it. In 'Jacques Audiard: contesting filiations', Julia Dobson moves from the centrality of the filial to Audiard's personal history – as the son of Michel Audiard, one of France's most successful scriptwriters, he was immersed in the world of film from an early age – to the thematic focus on the forging of a new identity by the central character of Audiard's acclaimed *De battre mon coeur s'est arrêté* (2005) 'against the familial and cultural discourses of patriarchal filiation'. Dobson sets out just how regularly and provocatively filiation has featured as a theme in contemporary French cinema before analysing how it functions as an 'auteurist trope' in Audiard's films, and how the opposing principles of the maternal and the paternal in *De battre mon coeur s'est arrêté* are successfully synthesised by the narrative's conclusion. Dysfunctional families and 'the incapacity of one generation to pass on anything positive to the next' are highlighted by Martin O'Shaughnessy as a recurrent preoccupation of the Dardenne brothers' four features, the last two of which have drawn direct attention to filiation by being entitled *Le Fils* and *L'Enfant*. O'Shaughnessy's reading of the Dardenne brothers' work argues that collectivity as a value in society is shown to be demolished in the brothers' documentaries, made before their feature films, and that 'the fictions pursue the study of a crisis of transmission in the narrower sphere of the family'. In so doing, and in their attempt to supply an ethics to fill the gap left by the disappearance of a 'totalising leftist vision [that can] translate the social in universalising terms', they draw on biblical stories and mythical representations of monstrous fathers such as Kronos. There are strong parallels between the visions of society depicted by the Dardenne brothers and Michael Haneke, and Libby Saxton, like O'Shaughnessy, suggests in her reading of Haneke that his acute observations of 'fragile, transitory, liquid ethical bonds which survive in a diegetic reality where intersubjective relations are increasingly mediated by technology' is the most productive line of enquiry presently offered by his work. If *Code inconnu* and *Caché* focus particularly on the ambiguity and precariousness of social ties in contemporary European societies, Haneke's other two French language films, *La Pianiste* and *Le Temps du loup*, zoom in on the white, middle-class, nuclear family as the generating source of these uncertain, shifting bonds, and as 'the stage where apocalyptic scenarios are compulsively rehearsed'. Whether directly or by implication, all Haneke's films challenge normative conceptions of the family, revealing it, as Saxton concludes, to be 'a series of fluid relations and identifications structured and sundered by conflicting desires and fears'.

That the disintegration of the nuclear, heterosexual family should be a recurrent issue in the work of these four directors is intriguing, given their male gender. The initial choice of only male directors for this volume is of course not entirely fortuitous, but I should emphasise that it in no way indicates that I consider male directors to be somehow better qualified than female ones to be the *auteurs* of contemporary francophone cinema. During the preparation of this book, another volume of essays devoted to contemporary women directors has been being written for the 'French Film Directors' series, in which female *auteurs* are already strongly represented. So rather than feeling obliged to account for not adding to their number, I shall re-emphasise that although Ozon is the only director featured here whose films give pride of place to sexuality and gendered relations (also an area treated by Libby Saxton in her essay on Haneke), a very different type of masculine authorship (if it can be so labelled) emerges from this volume from that offered by the directors of the *nouvelle vague*, the movement that first launched the concept of the *auteur*. Geneviève Sellier's recent publication *La Nouvelle Vague, un cinéma au masculin singulier* (2005) highlights how the progressive integration of feminist approaches into research on French cinema is continuing to alter our perspective on the history of auteurism. The prominence of the themes of filiation and the 'de-patriarchalisation' of the family in the films of Audiard, the Dardenne brothers, Haneke and Ozon is another sign that the self-celebratory and romantic masculine vision of the male *auteur* associated with the 'jeunes Turcs' of the *nouvelle vague* now lies firmly in the past.

References

Andrew, Dudley (1993), 'The unauthorized auteur today', in Jim Collins *et al.* (eds), *Film Theory Goes to the Movies*, New York and London, Routledge.

Barthes, Roland (1977), 'The death of the author', in Stephen Heath (ed.), *Image, Music, Text*, London, Fontana Paperbacks, pp. 142–8.

Bernas, Steven (2002), *L'Auteur au cinéma*, Paris, L'Harmattan.

Comolli, Jean-Louis and Narboni, Jean (1969), 'Cinema/Ideology/Criticism', translated by Susan Bennett, in *Screen Reader 1: Cinema/Ideology/Politics*, London, The Society for Education in Film and Television, 1977.

Cook, Pam and Bernink, Mieke (eds) (1999), *The Cinema Book* (2nd edn), London, British Film Institute.

Corrigan, Timothy (1991), *A Cinema Without Walls: Movies and Culture After Vietnam*, London, Routledge.

Crofts, Stephen (1998), 'Concepts of national cinema', in John Hill and Pamela Church Gibson (eds), *The Oxford Guide to Film Studies*, Oxford, Oxford University Press, pp. 385–94.

De Baecque, Antoine (1997), 'Aux aguets: que reste-t-il de la politique des auteurs?', *Cahiers du cinéma*, 518 (November), 22–5.

Gerstner, David and Steiger, Janet (eds) (2003), *Authorship and Film*, London and New York, Routledge.

Jeancolas, Jean-Pierre (2005), 'The confused image of le jeune cinéma', *Studies in French Cinema*, 5:3, 157–61.

Jeancolas, Jean-Pierre, Meusy, Jean-Jacques and Pinel, Vincent (1996), *L'Auteur du film: description d'un combat*, Arles, Institut Lumière/Actes Sud.

Naremore, James (1990), 'Authorship and the cultural politics of film criticism', *Film Quarterly*, 44:1 (Fall), 14–22.

Powrie, Phil (ed.) (1999), *French Cinema in the 1990s: Continuity and Difference*, Oxford, Oxford University Press.

Prédal, René (2001), *Le Cinéma d'auteur, une vieille lune?* Paris, Editions du Cerf.

Prédal, René (2002), *Le Jeune Cinéma français*, Paris, Nathan/VUEF.

Sarris, Andrew (1968), *The American Cinema: Directors and Directions 1929–1968*, New York, Dutton.

Sellier, Geneviève (2005), *La Nouvelle Vague, un cinéma au masculin singulier*, CNRS Editions, Collection 'Cinéma et audiovisuel'.

Vincendeau, Ginette (2005), *La Haine*, Cine-Files French Film Guides, London and New York, I. B. Tauris and Co. Ltd.

Wright Wexman, Virginia (ed.) (2003), *Film and Authorship*, New Brunswick, New Jersey and London, Rutgers University Press.

1

Olivier Assayas and the cinema of catastrophe

Paul Sutton

In a now celebrated *Sight and Sound* essay on Olivier Assayas' tenth feature film *demonlover* (2002), Jonathan Romney reconsidered the review that he had submitted after the film's 2002 premiere at Cannes. He had originally decided that:

> *demonlover* is the latest victim of the French tradition whereby a highly respected director over-reaches drastically, eliciting press-show booing … His latest film …, is undoubtedly his most experimental – a polished, brassy cyber thriller that for the first hour dazzles with its bold conception, but then heads into impenetrable erotic-thriller territory. Damned by its hybrid conception, it seems likely to be rejected by both ends of its possible audience: mainstream viewers will reject it as pretentious while Assayas' arthouse following may find it just plain tacky. (2002: 32)[1]

In his later reassessment, however, he suggested that the film wasn't simply a catastrophe but rather 'a film made in the catastrophic mode', arguing provocatively 'that a cinema truly attuned to our times can make sense only if it partakes of catastrophe, of a collapse of meaning' (2004: 28). Romney noted that the film's 'refusal to make sense' (2004: 28) could perhaps be understood in the broader context of Assayas' cinematic project, his 'critical discourse on cinema's current situation' (2004: 28). However, as the writer and director of a diverse range of films, which include the cult success *Irma Vep*

---

1 See Brunette (2003) and Stables (2004) for similar assessments of the film and Kenny (2003) and Smith (2002) for a more positive view of the film's 'devolve[ment] into something altogether more cerebral and abstract' (Kenny 2003: 19).

(1996), the documentary *HHH, portrait de Hou Hsiao Hsien* (1997), and the costume drama *Les Destinées sentimentales* (2000), as well as the controversial *demonlover* and the recent *Clean* (2004), Assayas' work has always sought, as Romney appears belatedly to acknowledge, to challenge cinematic convention.

While in some senses very obviously an *auteur* in the *Cahiers du cinéma* tradition, Assayas is a filmmaker who defies easy categorisation. He can be seen as an essayist of the cinema, concerned not only to examine the contemporary but also to explore the status and relationship of French cinema with its cinematic others. *Irma Vep*, for example, is an exploration and critique of the idea of cinematic authorship; it demonstrates the complicatedly collaborative nature of filmmaking and critiques through the director René Vidal (Jean-Pierre Léaud), the *auteur* that emerged with the French New Wave. As a film about the remaking of Louis Feuillade's *Les Vampires* (1915–16) for television, authorship and authorial integrity are repeatedly challenged. Much like *demonlover*, the film may be seen (in its conclusion at least), as a film partaking of a certain 'collapse of meaning'. It is precisely this idea of filmmaking in 'the catastrophic mode' that I wish to pursue in relation to Assayas' work, primarily through analyses of *demonlover* and *Irma Vep*, although I will look at a number of other representative films. Romney's assessment of *demonlover*'s potentially radical *modus operandi* is especially provocative when considered in relation to certain of the writings of Jean Baudrillard, a theorist whose connection to Assayas is not as surprising as it might at first seem, given the influence of Situationism on them both. However, before seeking to explore this idea of what one might call 'catastrophe cinema' in more detail, an account of the development of Assayas' career is necessary, not least because so many of his formative influences remain crucial to an understanding of his cinematic output.

It is well known that Assayas wrote extensively for *Cahiers du cinéma* in the late 1970s and early 1980s before moving on to write and direct his first feature film, *Désordre*, in 1986, a narrative trajectory made familiar by Godard, Truffaut and the other 'young Turks' of the *nouvelle vague* in the mid to late 1950s; however, the fact that he was employed to write for the magazine specifically as a filmmaker is perhaps less frequently acknowledged. As Assayas has himself recounted:

> I had been making short films. Daney and Toubiana saw them and asked me to write for the magazine. I had no background or even

interest in film theory then. I think that is what interested them. They wanted someone with a fresh approach to cinema'. (Daly 1999: 46)[2]

This distinction is of fundamental importance because it reveals the essential difference that Assayas wishes to point to between himself and an earlier generation of critics turned director/*auteur*; however, it also underpins Assayas' most firmly held beliefs about the cinema and artistic creation (strongly inflected by Situationism and the theoretical writings of Guy Debord). For Assayas (who despite his professed ignorance has become a remarkably astute film theoretician), the relationship between theory and practice is central to his understanding of what it means to be a filmmaker.[3]

Assayas' autobiographical *Une adolescence dans l'après-Mai: Lettre à Alice Debord*, written in 2002 and published in 2005, begins with the following reminiscence:

> Alice, l'autre soir, alors qu'on dînait chez toi, tu m'as demandé ce qui m'avait conduit là ... par quelles voies en suis-je venu à me passioner très jeune pour les thèses situationnistes ... et pourquoi l'oeuvre de Guy Debord m'aura tellement marqué, voire déterminé. (Assayas 2005: 1)[4]

The book articulates Assayas' response to the question posed by Alice Debord, describing his family background and the determining influences of his adolescence (he was thirteen in May 1968): George Orwell, Jerry Rubin, Abby Hoffman, a passion for London and Punk Rock and a decisive encounter with Situationism while at university.[5]

---

2 See also Kohn (1991) and Erickson (1997). Daney became chief editor of *Cahiers du cinéma* in 1974 and began to move the magazine away from 'the high political and psychoanalytic film theory [of] the 1970s back towards a more accessible cinephile approach informed by questions of history and culture' (Williams 2004: 265). For an account of Daney's career and an assessment of his significant contribution to film culture in post-War France see Williams (2004).

3 This particular subject is one that Assayas returns to frequently in interviews and articles; see, in particular, Daly (1999), Loiselle (1992), McGavin (1999), Peranson (1999), Peranson (2003) and Thoret (2005).

4 'Alice, the other evening, while we were dining at your place, you asked me what had led me here ... how had I come to be fascinated, while still so young, by Situationist theory ... and why the work of Guy Debord had marked, even determined me'. Unless otherwise stated all translations are my own.

5 Referring to London, Assayas comments: 'Il y avait là ... quelque chose du programme politique que j'avais ressenti comme central à Mai 68 et que je n'avais trouvé formulé nulle part'; 'There was there ... something of the political

Assayas recounts viewing the films of René Viénet and later discovering Debord's seminal *La Société du spectacle*:

> j'ai adopté ce livre comme point de départ, comme *ground zero*, de ma compréhension du monde en général et de la société où je vis en particulier; je n'en ai pas trouvé de plus convaincant. Ni avant, ni depuis'. (Assayas 2005: 71)[6]

The centrality of film culture to Assayas' life was impressed upon him somewhat closer to home. His father, Rémy Assayas, was a screenwriter who had worked as an assistant to Max Ophuls in the 1930s but who during the 1950s wrote screenplays for the cinema and then for television under the pseudonym Jacques Rémy (Assayas 2005: 11). Assayas would spend his summers gaining work experience on film sets and as his elderly father became increasingly ill began to work for him, helping him with his television scripts and eventually writing a number himself.[7] This led to Assayas producing scripts for friends who were directing short films; however, despite this background in scriptwriting Assayas' ambition lay in directing, 'mon désir profond était de réaliser' (Kohn 1991: 93)[8], and he was soon writing and directing his own short films.

La politique des auteurs

Assayas came, then, to writing film criticism and theory at *Cahiers du cinéma* already imbued with a strong directorial ambition, realised with the release of his debut feature *Désordre*. The film was a critical success, winning the critics prize at the 1986 Venice Film Festival,

---

programme that I had felt was central to May 1968 and which I hadn't found expressed anywhere else' (Assayas 2005: 24).

6 'I adopted this book as a point of departure, as *ground zero*, for my understanding of the world in general and of the society in which I lived in particular; I have never found anything more convincing. Neither before nor since'. Assayas, with Luc Barnier, has been involved in the re-release of Debord's films on DVD and in theatres; see *Cahiers du cinéma* (2005) for a comprehensive interview with Assayas on this subject.

7 With Claude Barma, Assayas' father adapted, until his death in 1981, George Simenon's Maigret novels for a long-running television series, *Les Enquêtes du commissaire Maigret* (1967–90). See Bandis and Martin (1998) and Kohn (1991) for accounts of this early period in Assayas' career.

8 'My deepest desire was to direct'.

occasioning favourable reviews in *Positif* and *Cahiers du cinéma* and establishing Assayas as a determined and ambitious *auteur*.[9] In a narrative that explores the Dostoevsky-like effects of a crime – a burglary that has escalated to murder – on a nascent young rock group, *Désordre* examines the gradual disintegration of the friendships that have held the band together, charting their struggle to deal with the weight of guilt and secrecy that envelops them. The film's milieu is one to which Assayas has returned in his most recent release *Clean*, set once again in and around the fringes of the international music scene, but it also reprises the subject matter of two of his four short films, *Rectangle – Deux chansons de Jacno* (1980) and *Winston Tong en studio* (1984).[10] *Désordre* introduces a number of distinctive traits that reoccur in later Assayas films such as 'sombre lighting, hyperactive camera movement, and extensive use of long takes' (Erickson 1997: 6). Assayas' ability to convey a sense of energy, vibrancy and tension while at the same time achieving an almost languorous pacing is remarkable and can be seen across his work, whether overtly as in *Irma Vep* or invisibly (almost as a sensation) in *Les Destinées sentimentales*, a film that despite appearing to be the most conventional of all of Assayas' films is in fact as challenging as any of them. *Désordre* (and his next two features) is also notable for its use of the silver retention process, made recognisable by its employment in David Fincher's *Seven* (1995 US), producing a noir-ish colour scheme, enhancing the dark blues and blacks that subsequently dominate this moralistic film.

To return to the question of writing, it is clear that whether for *Cahiers du cinéma* or for cinema and television, writing has been particularly important for Assayas. Working primarily in a French context and having only ever directed his own scripts he has strong views on the need for directors to write their own films, suggesting that the Hollywood model, whereby directors generally film scripts written by 'professional' scriptwriters, produces 'illustrators' rather than 'painters' (Kohn 1991: 96). While he admits that such a system can and has produced notable, even great 'illustrators', he argues that

9 See Ramasse (1987), Cazals (1986), Cazals and Philippon (1986) and Horvilleur (1986).

10 Music is vitally important to Assayas not only in terms of the creative use he makes of it in his films (he famously remastered the Sonic Youth soundtrack to *demonlover*), but also as a formative influence; see Assayas (2005) and Frodon (2004).

it is a very different type of creation to that which he is involved in: 'Je ne crois pas beaucoup au scénario "de scénariste". Pour moi, le scénario est avant tout l'émanation du désir d'un réalisateur' (Kohn 1991: 93).[11] This is, perhaps, an expression of the familiar difference between an *auteur* and a *metteur en scène*, which positions Assayas very much in the camp of the auteurists of the French New Wave.[12] Assayas has certainly made his views on cinematic authorship very clear:

> Comme tout le monde, j'ai des idées sur la théorie des auteurs. ... Le problème de l'attribution du film, dès lors qu'il est oeuvre d'art, est résolu. Le réalisateur en est le responsable. ... Il est clair que le metteur en scène, et lui seul, contrôle les tenants et les aboutissants des éléments disparates qui, réunis et organisés, constituent un tout qu'on appelle le cinéma. (Assayas 1983: 23).[13]

However, he remains distrustful of the *politique des auteurs*, and in particular of the canon of classical Hollywood directors that it championed – he has criticised academic film studies for setting in stone classical Hollywood as the only period worthy of study, the result of an 'historic cinephilia', which has mummified certain filmmakers and excluded others (Thoret 2005: 15).[14] Assayas is a filmmaker who believes fundamentally in the creative vision of the director (as writer too, it should be stressed) while at the same time recognising the collaborative dimension of the filmmaking process:

> Le cinéma hollywoodien des *blockbusters* est devenu collectif dans le sens où celui qui réalise un film comme *The Island*, en l'occurrence Michael Bay, n'est présent que sur une fraction du tournage effectif ... Si on adopte une grille auteuriste à l'ancienne [pour regarder les films

11 'I don't really believe in the "screenwriter's" script. For me the script comes first and foremost from the desire of a director'.
12 Assayas has said in interview: 'I'm very orthodox in my theories about auteurism. I'm not interested in films, I'm interested in people making films. I care more for a failed film by somebody I care about than a successful film by somebody I don't care about' (McGavin 1999: 55).
13 'Like everyone I have thoughts on the *auteur* theory ... The issue of the attribution of a film, as a work of art, has been settled. The director is the person responsible ... It is clear that the director, and he alone, controls the ins and outs of the disparate elements, which combined and organised, constitute the entity that we call the cinema'.
14 See Thoret (2005) for a detailed exploration of Assayas' views on cinematic authorship, classical Hollywood cinema and film theory; see Naremore (2004) for a recent reassessment of authorship.

américains d'aujourd'hui], on risque de passer à côté de beaucoup de choses, ou alors d'être dupe de faux-semblants. (Thoret 2005: 18)[15]

Many of Assayas' films are concerned explicitly with the question of authorship, seeking to engage critically with artistic creation, whether literary as in the case of *Fin août, début septembre* (1999) or cinematic as in *Irma Vep*.[16]

Fin août, début septembre and *Irma Vep*

Structured by a series of fades to black *Fin août, début septembre* is divided into chapters that span a year, the period between the end of August and the beginning of the following September. The film examines the almost imperceptible shift from late youth to early middle age, the gradual replacement of idealism by realism, freedom by responsibility.[17] As Peranson has suggested:

> In *Fin août*, the issue is no longer exploring the conflict between ideals and reality, but coming to terms with the contemporary world while remaining faithful to the values one continually is choosing to assume as one's own'. (1999: 66)

At the film's centre is the minor novelist Adrien (François Cluzet), the character around whom the others rotate. Suffering from the recurrence of an ultimately fatal illness, Adrien looks back on his life, provoking those around him to reassess their own lives.[18] The film has

15 'The Hollywood blockbuster has become a collective enterprise because the director of a film like *The Island*, Michael Bay, is only present for a fraction of the overall shoot ... If one adopts a traditional auteurist approach [to contemporary American films], one risks either passing a great deal by or being taken in by the fakes'.
16 It could be argued that *Les Destinées sentimentales* and *Clean* are also concerned with 'authorship', insofar as both films explore forms of artistic expression. See Brett (2001) for the view that the theme of craftsmanship versus commerce expressed in *Les Destinées sentimentales*, mirrors the 'painter' versus 'illustrator' distinction proposed by Assayas (Kohn 1991).
17 The film is concerned in a sense with the passage of time itself; it is marked perhaps by an almost Proustian sensibility.
18 Assayas has spoken of how he developed the outline for *Fin août* after experiencing the death of a number of friends from AIDS. In the same interview he discusses the impression that the death of Serge Daney made on him and agreed that 'Serge's death was one part of what inspired the character of Adrien' (Daly 1999: 44).

been seen by many critics as autobiographical insofar as it describes characters and is set in a milieu that is especially familiar to Assayas; it is also self-critical in its exploration of authorship and artistic influence. Despite its focus on relationships and its affective power, the film puts into play a number of Assayas' theoretical and artistic concerns, ideas that emerge from his engagement with Situationism and the work of Henri Lefebvre to the influence of artists and writers such as Joseph Beuys, David Hockney and Marcel Proust.[19]

As one critic has remarked of Assayas' films, 'scenes always start *in media res*, ... there's never any buildup or background detail to take you outside the immediacy of the emotional material onscreen' (Jones 1996: 51); this is true of *Irma Vep* and it is especially true of *Fin août*, where the elliptical narrative is key to the film's emotional and theoretical impact. As Assayas has explained:

> This elliptical way of telling the story is a way of communicating with the audience, of giving the space for the viewer to project himself into the story and recreating his own thoughts of it. Like in a novel. When you're reading a novel you are creating the images, directing it somehow. I think that in a film you can ultimately try and get a relationship with the viewer as close as the novel has with the reader'. (Peranson 1999: 69)

The importance of writing, and of authorship, for Assayas is evidently a central concern of *Fin août*, offering the spectator an insight into the working through of his theoretical ideas and their practical, textual and cinematic application.

By contrast, as a film that charts the difficulties that beset a film crew remaking Feuillade's serial *Les Vampires* for television, *Irma Vep* explores the question of authorship in the context of a form of filmmaking that is more or less antithetical to any traditional notion of the *auteur*.[20] The remake occupies a somewhat troubled site in French cinema, where remakes are generally seen as commercially exploitative, inferior copies which have the unfortunate effect of 'reducing

19 A Beuys sketch features in the film and Assayas has noted that Hockney's Polaroid photomontages were a source for the fragmented 'snapshot' structure of the film.

20 Interestingly, Assayas himself apparently looked at the possibility of a TV version of *Les Vampires*, but 'never got past the planning point' (Morrison 1997: 63).

the French original to a popular copy' (Mazdon 1999: 223).[21] Remakes challenge the sanctity of the signed original and undermine the *auteur*'s stamp of creative individuality. In *Irma Vep*, Assayas explores the strategies adopted by the characters within the film to respond to the anxieties that the remake project generates for them, while at the same time playing self-consciously with the question of cinematic authorship. Thus the film contains two directors, René Vidal (Jean-Pierre Léaud) and José Murano (Lou Castel), from not too dissimilar filmic backgrounds, seeking to reinterpret the work of a third director, Louis Feuillade, while also trying to reconfigure the original heroine/star, Irma Vep/Musidora, for a contemporary audience. By staging the difficulties that confront these various *auteurs*, Assayas is able to produce a film, under his own authorial control, that subjects authorship itself to critical analysis.

There is little doubt that *Irma Vep* is itself what might generally be referred to as an *auteur* film. Its production history, authorial signature and attendance figures appear to confirm its designation, and even the fact that it achieved a certain cult status in the United States, which enabled it to achieve a far wider audience than expected (it was also Assayas' breakthrough film in terms of the US market), serves only to reinforce its *auteur* cinema status.[22] However, elements of the film's style and its explicit intertextual referencing, and occasional adoption of, alternative forms of cinema – commercial, political and historical – combine to produce a film that perhaps simultaneously escapes the narrow confines of its purely *auteur* origins. *Irma Vep*'s opening shot features two telephone conversations that serve to situate the diegetic film, but which also offer an ironic commentary on Assayas' own '*auteur*' film. In the first the production manager (Alex Descas) is discussing percentage returns and amortisation (reminiscent of the cheque writing credit sequence in Godard's *Tout Va Bien*, 1972); in the second a switchboard operator (Estelle Larrivaz) is explaining that: 'It's an art movie, yeah. It's cultural, along the lines of ... You'll have all the guarantees you need. No, there's no need to

21 Mazdon notes that contrary to popular belief it is frequently the popular genres, such as comedy, that are remade in Hollywood not the *auteur*/art film. In other words, as she argues, 'it is not French "art" which is under threat from the remake, but rather those popular domestic genres which are themselves dismissed by many French critics' (1999: 224).

22 In an international context 'one of the most successful of French cinema's marketing strategies has been the notion of the *auteur*' (Powrie 1999: 8).

worry. He's a good director. You've heard of him'. While she speaks she plays with a revolver, a prop. Shortly afterwards Maggie Cheung makes her entrance, more or less unnoticed by the office staff, but prefigured nonetheless in the opposition set up between the label 'art movie' and the generic associations that the symbolism of the pistol targets.

The casting of Maggie Cheung (the film was written by Assayas specifically for Cheung) is central to *Irma Vep*'s project to consider the status of French cinema in relation to its cinematic others – Hollywood and Asian cinema – while at the same time reconsidering the role of the *auteur* in contemporary French cinema. Cheung is both the character Maggie, reprising within the remake the role of Irma Vep played originally by the French silent star Musidora, but also at the same time Maggie Cheung the international star of the Hong Kong action movie.[23] Described as being 'as fast paced and hip as a Hong Kong action film' (Erickson 1997: 6), aspects of *Irma Vep*'s visual style draw upon the genres associated with Cheung and evidenced not only in the clip from *The Heroic Trio* (Johnny To, 1992) that Assayas uses, but also expressed in sequences such as the 'burglary' episode, where Cheung as Cheung becomes Irma Vep and steals a necklace from a room in the hotel in which she is staying. Maggie Cheung's Chinese origins and her English schooling place her on a kind of racial borderline (she speaks Mandarin, Cantonese and English), in the same way perhaps that her various and numerous film roles place her on a number of generic borderlines. A major star throughout Asia and Europe, Cheung's cinematic identity is a complex and fluid one.[24] It is precisely this borderline status that appeals to Vidal, the director of *Les Yeux qui fascinent* (episode six of Feuillade's serial, translated generally as *Hypnotic Eyes*), the film within Assayas' film. It is both her difference and her familiarity that make her ideal for the role of Irma Vep, an impossible role for a French actress, Vidal argues, given the mythic status of Musidora in French cinema, a status that relies on her star persona, her signature style.

Maggie Cheung functions, then, both as a signifier for another genre, another style, while at the same time forging a new role for

23 Essentially Vidal is remaking the character Irma Vep as opposed to *Les Vampires* itself.

24 Ciecko and Lu argue that Cheung has a 'fluid pan-Asian cinematic identit[y]' and a 'complex relationship to notions of Chineseness' (1999: 72).

herself in the West and simultaneously updating, modernising, a classic role, that of Irma Vep. Cheung's triple identity enables Assayas to pose questions that relate to authorial singularity, while also allowing him to incorporate the popular, the new, the different into *Irma Vep*.[25] Cheung offers a counter to the view expressed by the 'journalist who loves John Woo' (Antoine Basler) who interviews her in *Irma Vep*. It is in this sequence that the debate around French cinema and its cinematic others, here Hong Kong cinema, is most clearly expressed. The views of this journalist, identified purely in relation to his cinematic tastes, are according to Assayas 'taken almost word for word from things I've heard Matthieu Kassovitz [director of *La Haine*, 1995] say' (Erickson 1997: 7).[26] The journalist is aggressive and self-promoting, foregrounded ironically in Maggie's assertion (in response to a demand for her view) that John Woo is 'so masculine'; Cheung is also marginalised visually at this point (she was devalued as simple spectacle before the interview even began: 'Oh, elle est belle ... You look beautiful'). In the early part of the interview the camera circles around Cheung and the interviewer, observing coldly, and then as Maggie is asked about French cinema a pan from the interviewer to Maggie serves perhaps as a visual reminder of the distance between the two film cultures being discussed.

Assayas' self-conscious and self-reflexive film explores, then, a set of oppositions: *auteur* versus *metteur en scène*, 'painter' versus 'illustrator', avant-garde versus mainstream cinema, France or Europe versus its cinematic others (Hong Kong and Hollywood), and perhaps even film history versus film theory; oppositions that are expressed not only through the apparent failure of the director within the film to effectively reproduce Feuillade (arguably an example of filmmaking in the 'catastrophic mode'), but also through the conflictual and complex cultural and personal relationships represented within the narrative.[27]

---

25 Cheung has been involved in 'artistic' films, part of Hong Kong's second wave New Wave, as well as acting in commercial and popular cinema, for which she had been known in the West (until the relative success of *Irma Vep*); she is now an international star.

26 Assayas continues, 'I think a lot of Hong Kong films are aesthetically interesting, but they're successful with American audiences for all the wrong reasons' (Erickson 1997: 7).

27 The historical dimensions of the film take in Feuillade clearly, but there are explicit references to the New Wave and to the political filmmakers of the left-bank also.

These binaries serve to raise a number of significant questions for French cinema, in particular how to deal with the legacy of the *nouvelle vague*. Both of the diegetic directors, Vidal and his replacement Murano, try to explore the relationship between early and contemporary cinema, addressing in particular the difficulty of producing a so-called 'original' film given the weighty legacy of French cinematic history. This tension is represented by the remake project itself and in the different approaches that these two directors adopt. Vidal, the *auteur* (a *nouvelle vague* connection made explicit by the casting of Jean-Pierre Léaud, child star of Truffaut's *Les Quatre Cents Coups*, 1959), is paralysed by the authorial legacy of Feuillade and by a desire to recapture a moment of lost cinematic origin (he undergoes a breakdown in the film that literalises the cultural anxieties expressed in it, a literal collapse); Murano, by contrast, 'coded for us as an erstwhile political director by the inscription "Chiapas" across the back of his bright orange jacket' (Morrison 1997: 64), just needs the money. The crisis that faces these two directors – stasis on the one hand, selling out on the other – dramatises what Assayas sees as the contradictions inherent in the 'end of cinema' argument:

> I think that the *nouvelle vague* generation ... consider themselves as the last possible filmmakers, because they are stuck in their generation's vision: there first was classic cinema, then there was 'post-classic' cinema, which is their cinema, modern cinema, and then there's ... nothing else. (Peranson 2003: 13)

For Assayas the problem that faces many filmmakers of his generation lies in the fact that they have not produced their own dialogue with cinema history but have instead looked back to the New Wave filmmakers, who themselves had a very specific relationship with classical Hollywood cinema. Assayas argues of his peers that:

> they were using the same blueprint instead of defining their own. Except time had passed and what was once a creative, lively, challenging dialectic became some kind of common wisdom, an academic empty shell. Which is the fate of any theory outlasting its time. So post-*nouvelle vague* filmmakers ended up as seeing themselves – and being seen by traditionalist film theory – as *post-cinema*, or as dealing with the ruins of cinema. (Peranson 2003: 13)

Thus Assayas, and Vidal within *Irma Vep*, turns to inspiration from sources outside of classical Hollywood cinema, looking instead to other radical and experimental precursors. Thus in *Irma Vep*, Vidal produces a radical non-narrative reinterpretation of *Les Vampires* for a contemporary audience with his extremely short 'Lettrist' scratch film, *Les Yeux qui fascinent*.[28] He moves from a simple and faithful remake, 'just images, no soul' he complains, to an avant-garde film that ironically also captures something of the dynamism, energy and spectacle of the popular, commercial Hong Kong film *The Heroic Trio*, the film that had inspired Vidal to cast Maggie Cheung as Irma Vep in the first place.[29] Vidal's film subverts the safety of the traditional remake, replacing it instead with a 'catastrophic' film, the product of his own personal collapse in the face of the critical *catastrophe* that the remake was in danger of becoming. Much like Assayas' *demonlover*, Vidal's film turns the remake back on itself in a gesture of Baudrillardian provocation. Conforming perhaps to Baudrillard's description of catastrophe as 'acceleration, precipitation, excess' (Guillemot and Soutif in Gane 1993: 43), Vidal's *Les Yeux qui fascinent* ultimately reveals the vacuity of the diegetic film's original remake project.

What Assayas achieves in *Irma Vep* is the production of a fierce, yet darkly comic, critique of French cinema, the New Wave, the *auteur*, while at the same time proposing a way out of the impasse before which French film has foundered. Assayas ends his film about cinematic conflict and failure on a powerfully upbeat note. Through a kind of *bricolage* of avant-garde and commercial cinema and early and contemporary film he produces an imaginative and inspiring experimental film that rebuts the suggestion that post New Wave French cinema is dead; as Chris Darke has noted:

28 This avant-garde sequence is reputedly a homage to Isidore Isou's *Venom and Eternity* (Jones 1997: 37).

29 *The Heroic Trio* is a film that appears to differ somewhat from standard Hong Kong genre film in so far as it privileges women. However, as critics have pointed out, and as Cheung herself has noted both in interviews and within Assayas' film (in the John Woo interview sequence), one of the dimensions lost in the globalisation (i.e. Hollywood-isation) of the Hong Kong action film is precisely 'the richness and ambiguity of gendered representations' (Ciecko and Lu 1999: 72). Thus '[I]n terms of gender, one factor which has consistently marked Hong Kong action film narratives in recent decades is a crisis of masculinity and a subversion of the conventions of heterosexual romance' (Ciecko and Lu 1999: 72). *The Heroic Trio* may be thought of as a spectacular film for a number of reasons: it is flagrantly narcissistic in terms of its technical virtuosity, combining fantastic lighting, fast editing, extensive wire work and a range of overt special effects.

Assayas succeeds where the fictional Vidal fails because he can use
Vidal as a surrogate conscience to shoulder the weight of film history
for him. Where Vidal is creatively exhausted by his fidelity to the
past, Assayas can be an urgent force. *Irma Vep* doesn't work out its
mourning for cinema with the romantic nostalgia of Godard's *Le
Mépris* or *Passion*, it's more like the Mexican Day of the Dead: remem-
brance as an act of celebration'. (1997: 52)

What Assayas also accomplishes with this dynamic 'scratch' film is an
articulation of his beliefs regarding the relationship between theory
and practice, and it is surely no accident that he chooses a Lettrist film
to represent this. As will become clear in the next section the Situa-
tionists, so central to Assayas' conception of filmmaking, emerged out
of the Lettrist International in the late 1950s.[30]

Film theory and practice

As *Fin août, début septembre* and *Irma Vep* demonstrate, Assayas
has an especially complex relationship with notions of authorship.
He has allied himself to a particular perspective in both theoretical
and practical terms yet he is acutely aware of the dangers of a theory
that has, in his view, been co-opted by academia. It is here that a
number of issues that are key for Assayas begin to coalesce. Assayas
holds a particular position on the importance of theory for cinema,
not only in terms of the theory or criticism associated with publications like *Cahiers du cinéma* and the work of academics in disciplines
such as film studies, but also in terms of the fundamental relationship between the theory and practice that, in his view, underpins all
creative endeavour. In his remarkably frank and detailed interview
with Mark Peranson, Assayas began to make a connection between
his understanding of the relationship between theory and practice
and that between writing and directing in his filmmaking:

30 See Debord (1955). The Lettrist group, led by Isidore Isou, was renowned
for its physical manipulation of found film footage, which also involved the
addition of text and soundtracks in order to subvert the original meaning.
For texts relating to the Lettrist International and the Situationist International see
'Debordiana' at www.chez.com/debordiana/debordiana.htm; see also http://
libcom.org/library/internationale-situationiste, www.nothingness.org/SI/ and
www.notbored.org/LI.html (all accessed 22/04/06).

The cinema I relate to is a cinema *that is about questioning cinema*, one that has never been satisfied with the usual answers. And this is not only about images, it's also about writing, maybe mostly about writing. When I'm talking about theory and practice, I realize that I'm actually talking about the process of writing and then directing, which is very similar. I hadn't thought about it before, but I'm just thinking about it while we're talking, maybe the way theory has been cut from practice is similar to the way writing has been cut off from directing. (Peranson 2003: 12–13)

Reversing the move that Assayas makes here, I would like to move on to consider his very particular relation with film theory and the importance of the theory/practice dialectic for his work, a concern that results directly from his engagement with Situationism and the writings of Guy Debord.[31] As noted previously Assayas has become an astute theorist of the cinema; however, he has consistently sought to distance himself from theory based within an institutional, academic context; seeking rather to articulate a form of theory more closely connected to the object of study itself, one that paradoxically seeks not to distance itself critically but rather to engage through a form of practice-based theoretical reflection:

Le problème, aujourd'hui, c'est que la réflexion est considérée comme une activité honteuse, on valorise au contraire une pratique instinctive, ... qui serait garante d'une forme d'authenticité. Bref, la théorie est jugée stérile ... Mais enfin, quelles qu'en soit les raisons, on baigne hélas dans cette idéologie-là; une opposition binaire qui, à mon sens, cache le discours de la domination. Celui du pouvoir, celui de l'argent, et qui, faute de pouvoir être formulé, se dissimule sous le masque du surtout non-dit ... Là où il aurait fallu choisir les artistes, la théorie du cinéma a choisi les professeurs'. (Thoret 2005: 16)[32]

31 'To me theory is worthless if it is not connected to practice. I guess it's the one essential thing I've learned from my reading of Guy Debord, everything else stems from it. To me theory is some kind of praxis, really, it's useless otherwise. I'm not interested in this notion of film criticism, I'm interested in *film theory*, in a constant dialogue between film theory and film practice' (Peranson 2003: 8).

32 The problem today is that reflection is considered a shameful activity; an instinctive practice is valorised instead, ... which is seen as the guarantor of a form of authenticity. Essentially, theory is judged to be sterile ... But ultimately, whatever the reasons, we are steeped in this ideology, a binary opposition that to my mind hides the dominant discourse: the discourse of power and of money, which as a result of its formulation, hides behind the mask of the unsaid, the instinctive

It is perhaps interesting to note that within academic film studies
there has been a return recently to 'thinkers' or theorists who were
also filmmakers, working and writing in the 1920s and 1930s, a recognition perhaps of the issues being considered here by Assayas.[33] There
is undoubtedly a certain ambivalence in his views on the relationship between theory and practice, evident in his concern to avoid the
valorisation of a purely instinctive practice; however, he stresses that
'when theory is not in relationship to the most immediate practice,
then it just does not work' (Peranson 2003: 11). Assayas' films are
in many ways 'theoretical' films and yet a certain lightness of touch
ensures that they are rarely didactic or sterile exercises. Situationism
as a theory is also fundamentally a 'practice' and it is clearly this that
struck a chord with the adolescent Assayas, growing up in the post
May 1968 period. Assayas' interest in music, and punk rock in particular, coincides with his theoretical investment in Situationism; thus
the emergence of punk, for Assayas, gave rise to:

> quelques mois de confusion où l'on a senti les choses vaciller, un bref
> moment sinon tout en tout cas beaucoup aura été possible et il a été
> donné à chacun de pouvoir se reformuler. (Assayas 2005: 86)[34]

Assayas even goes so far as to argue that punk rock could perhaps
be seen as representing a quasi-situationism: 'je dis situation avec
beaucoup de précaution mais assez sérieusement ... Il n'y avait pas
énormément de pensée, mais il y avait cette chose précieuse: de la
pratique' (2005: 87).[35]

For Assayas the question became how to reproduce the energy,
the intensity, the presentness of punk cinematically, and as noted
earlier it was in the context of the post-punk New Wave in France that
Assayas produced his short films. Filmmaking in Assayas' account
offered him an opportunity, through the solitary activity of writing on
the one hand, and the collective experience of shooting on the other,
to articulate cinematically his desire to connect critically with the

... In this context, where it should have chosen the artists, film theory chose the
professors'.

33 See for example, Moore (1999).

34 'A couple of months of confusion during which one felt things waver, a brief
moment during which, if not everything, at least a great deal seemed possible
and everybody was in a position to remake themselves'.

35 'I say situation with a great deal of caution but seriously nonetheless ... There
wasn't a great deal of thinking, but there was this precious thing: practice'.

world around him. Assayas describes shooting the party sequence in *L'Eau froide* (1994), his contribution to the celebrated series of French television films *Tous les garçons et les filles de leur âge*, as a moment of profound realisation. The one hour long films were commissioned by Arte, who required them to be 'autobiographical, to concentrate on the directors' teenage years, and to include a party scene and popular songs from the relevant period' (Everett 1999: 49).[36] Shooting the party sequence becomes, Assayas argues, 'une sorte de *happening*' (2005: 91), prompting him to wonder, 'dans quelle mesure les tournages de films ..., ne sont-ils pas des *situations*? Ne relèvent-ils pas de la création consciente dans le domaine de la vie quotidienne?' (2005: 92).[37] He summarises his philosophy *vis-à-vis* his own practice by suggesting that ultimately:

> En ce qui me concerne, je n'ai plus jamais vu la fabrication des films autrement, c'est-à-dire comme un double mouvement, celui de l'incarnation de l'écriture – plus intime, c'est là que se constitue le sens – et celui de l'action où, hors du sens justement, se constituent jour de tournage après jour de tournage les fragments d'une pratique d'un art global inextricablement fondu dans le réel'. (Assayas 2005: 93)[38]

Of all Assayas' films *demonlover* has proved to be the most controversial and it is seen by many critics as his most overtly theoretical.[39] The film became notorious not only for its portrayal of the world of internet pornography and corporate intrigue but more contentiously for its apparent descent into incomprehensibility in its second half. In conclusion, it is to this aspect of the film's reception that I now wish to turn.

36 Assayas' film was one of three films also shot as features and released cinematically.
37 'To what extent are film shoots ... *situations*? Are they not part of conscious creation, part of everyday life?'.
38 'As far as I'm concerned, I've never thought of filmmaking as anything but a double movement, embodied in writing – more intimate, where meaning is formed – and in practice, where, beyond meaning in fact, the fragments of a global art inextricably cast from the real are put together during one day's filming after another'.
39 See, for example, Peranson (2003).

Conclusion: the cinema of catastrophe

Elizabeth Walden has suggested that to argue that *demonlover* operates in a catastrophic mode is to misrepresent the film and to 'risk missing the complex and complexly meaningful experience' the film provides (2005: 1). While reports on the unintelligibility of *demonlover* have certainly been exaggerated, the film is nonetheless marked by a strategy of resistance that Walden's critique does not allow for. By recuperating the film, 'as critique', Walden undermines the full power of its radical potential. According to Jean Baudrillard, traditional forms of criticism, traditional modes of critical thinking (dialectical and critical theory) are no longer sufficient to confront the dominant discourses of twenty-first century industrialised society; thus he argues that:

> 'Whereas before we were in the crisis of reality, the crisis of efficiency, the crisis of values ..., now we are in a stage of catastrophe in its literal sense, in other words it's not exactly an apocalypse but a form of catastrophe and we don't really have the conceptual and analytical principles to confront it... because all our thinking is itself formed in negativity, in criticism, in traditional analysis'. (Sutton 1997: 223)

Assayas shares with Debord the view that 'si l'art ne pouvait plus souscrire à la société et à son nouvel ordre, s'il ne pouvait plus en être le miroir il lui incombait d'en être la contradiction radicale' (Assayas 1995: 47).[40] Initially, *demonlover* does not appear to be so much a contradiction as a confirmation of contemporary corporate society, it appears fatally complicit (as many reviewers have argued) with the glossy, amoral, corporate world it represents; however, it is precisely in its exaggerated, excessive presentation of this world that the film achieves its 'contradiction radicale'. Assayas has described how the film is designed to become unintelligible, unreadable, enigmatic, a strategy that echoes Baudrillard's appeal for *la pensée radicale*, for radical thought. Thus Assayas explains:

> what I am trying to do is establish this post-Hitchcockian thriller mood, and then ... then I just blow the whole thing up. We are in this process where we think we know what's going on, where we're heading, except gradually we realise something's wrong. You know that story, I know

40 'If art can no longer subscribe to society and to its new order, if it can no longer be its mirror, then it is incumbent upon it to be its radical contradiction'.

that story, instead of going through it once more what I'm going to do is break this dramaturgic mode ... the manipulative conventions of *safe* storytelling. (Peranson 2003: 4)

Safe storytelling is too familiar, is too critically complicit with the object of criticism; truly radical thought, as Baudrillard has argued, 'lies in the intersection between meaning and non-meaning' (1995: 55). Thus, *demonlover* may be read as a film that breaks consciously with accepted patterns of narrative causality, and undermines its own structural coherence as a provocation. As Baudrillard argues:

the absolute rule – that of symbolic exchange – is to render what is given you. Never less, always more. The absolute rule of thought is: render the world as it was given to us – unintelligible – and if possible, a little more unintelligible. A little more enigmatic. (1995: 62)

The 'catastrophic mode' adopted by Assayas' film might then offer an alternative to the traditional critical strategy defended by Walden and instead one might concur with Baudrillard when he argues that 'all radical criticism now belongs to the ... catastrophic' (cited in Sutton 1997: 192). But the final word ought perhaps to go to Jonathan Romney, with whom this all began:

demonlover manifestly doesn't 'work', but that's the point. Within the terms of Assayas' argument, a film that works would be the greatest catastrophe of all. (2004: 31)[41]

References

Assayas, O. (1983), 'Sur une politique', *Cahiers du cinéma*, 353 (November), 22–5.

Assayas, O. (1995), 'Guy Debord: dans des circonstances éternelles du fond d'un naufrage', *Cahiers du cinéma*, 487 (January), 46–9.

Assayas, O. (1998), 'Apropos of Maggie', translated by L. Mortimer, *Metro*, 113/114, 62–4.

Assayas, O. (2005), *Une adolescence dans l'après-Mai: lettre à Alice Debord*, Paris, Cahiers du cinéma.

41 See Romney (2004) for a detailed and very productive analysis of *demonlover*; other particularly useful critical explorations of the film include Maule (2005) and Walden (2005). Peranson (2003) provides the most comprehensive explanation (or defence) of the film by Assayas himself and is invaluable (my thanks to Mark Peranson for making a copy available to me).

Bandis, H., and Martin, A. (1998), 'The cinema according to Olivier Assayas', *Cinema Papers*, 126 (August), 32–5.

Baudrillard, J. (1995), 'Radical thought', translated by D. Macey, *Parallax*, 1 (September), 53–62.

Brett, A. (2001), '*Les Destinées sentimentales*', *Film Review*, 34 (February), 59.

Brunette, P. (2003), 'Slick surfaces and much confusion: Assayas' ambitious *demonlover*', *indieWIRE*, 22 September, www.indiewire.com/movies/movies_030922demon.html, accessed 08/01/06.

Cahiers du cinéma (2005), 'Les perruques de la gratitude: entretien avec Olivier Assayas', *Cahiers du cinéma*, 605 (October), 82–6.

Cazals, T. (1986), '*Désordre* d'Olivier Assayas: l'orage des sentiments', *Cahiers du cinéma*, 389 (November), 4–6.

Cazals, T., and Philippon, A. (1986), 'L'émotion pure: entretien avec Olivier Assayas', *Cahiers du cinéma*, 389 (November), 8–11.

Ciecko, A. T. and Lu, S. H. (1999), 'The heroic trio: Anita Mui, Maggie Cheung, Michelle Yeoh – self-reflexivity and the globalization of the Hong Kong action heroine', *Post Script*, 19:1, 70–86.

Daly, F. (1999), 'Critical instinct', *Film West*, 37 (July), 44–7.

Darke, C. (1997), 'Irma Vep', *Sight and Sound*, 7:3, 51–2.

Darke, C. (1999), 'Late August, Early September/Fin août, début septembre', *Sight and Sound*, 9:9 (September), 48.

Debord, G. (1955), 'Pourquoi le lettrisme', *Potlach*, 22 (September).

Erickson, S. (1997), 'Making a connection between the cinema, politics and real life: an interview with Olivier Assayas', *Cineaste*, 22:4, 6–9.

Frodon, J.-M. (2004), 'Olivier Assayas: la musique de Brian Eno pose des questions de cinéma', *Cahiers du cinéma*, 593 (September), 24–5.

Gane, M. (ed.) (1993), *Baudrillard Live: Selected Interviews*, London, Routledge.

Horvilleur, G. (1986), 'Les films du mois: *Désordre*', *Cinématographe*, 124 (November), 57.

Jones, K. (1996), 'Tangled up in blue: the cinema of Olivier Assayas', *Film Comment*, 32:1 (January/February), 51–7.

Jones, K. (1997), 'Night exterior', *Filmmaker*, 5:3, 36–7 and 76–7.

Kenny, G. (2003), '*demonlover*', *Première*, 17:2 (October), 19.

Kohn, O. (1991), 'Scénaristes et réalisateurs: trois *auteurs* français', *Positif*, 363 (May), 92–6.

Loiselle, M.-C. (1992), 'Entretien avec Olivier Assayas', *24 Images*, 59 (Winter), 53–6.

McGavin, P. Z. (1999), 'Fall colors', *Filmmaker*, 7:4 (Summer), 55–5, 77–8.

Maule, R. (2005), '*demonlover* (Olivier Assayas, 2002) as allegory of global corporate media', www.ncl.ac.uk/crif/sfc/downloads/conference/maule.doc, accessed 08/01/06.

Mazdon, L. (1999), 'Remaking paternity: *Mon Père ce héros* (Lauzier, 1991) and *My Father the Hero* (Miner, 1994)', in Phil Powrie (ed.), *French Cinema in the 1990s: Continuity and Difference*, Oxford, Oxford University Press, pp. 223–33.

Moore, R. (1999), *Savage Theory: Cinema as Modern Magic*, Durham, NC, Duke University Press.

Morrison, S. (1997), 'Irma Vep', *Cineaction*, 42, 63–5.

Naremore, J. (2004), 'Authorship', in T. Miller and R. Stam (eds), *A Companion to Film Theory*, Oxford, Blackwell, pp. 9–24.

Peranson, M. (1999), 'A conversation with Olivier Assayas on *Fin août, début septembre*', *Cineaction*, 48 (December), 66–72.

Peranson, M. (2003), 'Reattaching the broken thread: Olivier Assayas on filmmaking and film theory', *Cinema Scope*, 14 (Spring), 30–9.

Powrie, P. (1999), 'Heritage, history and "New Realism": French cinema in the 1990s', in P. Powrie (ed.), *French Cinema in the 1990s: Continuity and Difference*, Oxford, Oxford University Press, pp. 1–21.

Ramasse, F. (1987), '*Désordre*: Adam et Eve ont raté le précédent', *Positif*, 312 (February), 61–3.

Romney, J. (2002), 'Review of *demonlover*', *Screen International*, 1360 (21 June), 32.

Romney, J. (2004), 'Stop making sense', *Sight and Sound*, 14:5 (May), 28–31.

Smith, G. (2002), '21st century blues', *Film Comment*, 38:4 (July/August), www.filmlinc.com/fcm/7–8–2002/cannesgs.htm, accessed 14/04/06.

Stables, K. (2004), '*demonlover*', *Sight and Sound*, 14:5 (May), 52–3.

Sutton, P. (1997), 'Endangered species? An interview with Jean Baudrillard', *Angelaki*, 2:3, 217–24.

Thoret, J.-B. (2005), 'Tendances: conversation avec Olivier Assayas', *Panic*, 1 (November), 15–21.

Walden, E. (2005), '"You want to torture Zora?" Olivier Assayas's *demonlover* as critique', *New Cinemas: Journal of Contemporary Film*, 3:1, 55–66.

Williams, J. S. (2004), 'Debates 1960–2004: the exercise was beneficial, monsieur Daney', in M. Temple and M. Witt, *The French Cinema Book*, London, BFI, pp. 265–72.

2

Jacques Audiard: contesting filiations

Julia Dobson

After substantial success as a screenplay writer, Jacques Audiard has directed some of the most engaging and enduring films of the last decade in France. His films, *Regarde les hommes tomber* (1994), *Un héros très discret* (1996) and *Sur mes lèvres* (2001), received critical recognition, yet he is often absent from canon-forming lists of contemporary French directors. This will undoubtedly change to reflect the critical and popular acclaim afforded his most recent work to date, *De battre mon coeur s'est arrêté* (2005).

Audiard's work reflects several of the dominant preoccupations of contemporary French cinema: an engagement with realism (the phenomenon of the 'new new wave'), the interrogation of the construction of (cultural) memory, narratives of exclusion and *déliaison sociale* and a reassertion of the impact of the socio-economic on the personal in wide-ranging depictions of the workplace. While all of these themes remain familiar, Audiard's films counter the ultimately pessimistic tenor which often dominates such material with a structural, thematic and filmic insistence upon the enduring power of imagination, of fiction and of (re)invention. Audiard's films are populated by loners and outsiders; the structure and content of the narratives are centred on shifting and ambiguous dynamics of solitude and solidarity, the inescapable burden of the allotment of a social role and identity here offset by the ultimate empowerment of central characters to reinvent themselves and escape such constraints. The temporal and spatial tensions of these struggles are played out through and against generic schema, foregrounding the deliberate manipulation of the road movie (*Regarde les hommes tomber*), the heritage film (*Un héros très discret*) and the *polar* (*Sur mes lèvres*) in a style which combines an explicit mannerism and enjoyment of virtuoso set pieces with a visceral insistence upon the capacity for change and transformation.

Audiard's auteurist credentials are secure (his work is characterised by the recurrence of particular stylistic and thematic features across a range of generic frameworks), yet this traditional model of the *auteur* is inflected with the necessity of situating this work within wider contemporary cultural and political discourses. The later sections of this chapter will discuss the question of filiation as one which concerns the thematic focus of his films, narrative choices, generic adoptions and subversions, indeed the cinema and the filial are central to his personal history. Audiard's immersion in the world of cinema from a young age requires mention here; his father, Michel Audiard, was one of France's most prominent and successful scriptwriters. Audiard initially followed his father and his successful scriptwriting credits include: *Randonnée mortelle (Deadly Circuit*, 1983) written with his father, *Poussière d'ange (Killing Time*, 1987), *Swing Troubadour* (1991) and *Grosse Fatigue (Dead Tired*, 1994). He also worked in editing for six years, notably as assistant on Polanski's *The Tenant* (1976). His uncle is actor Maurice Biraud, his sister an editor and he is married to director Marion Vernoux. Despite this overwhelming personal cinematic background, Audiard attests to having become a filmmaker almost by accident 'without thinking, without realising and in no haste' (Baudry 2005), directing his first film at the age of forty. His position in general overviews of contemporary French cinema is characterised by the sense of a lack of fit with current trends. In Prédal's substantial study he is categorised as an awkward case in the (non) group of 'maniéristes et déviants' under a further subheading of 'anti-realists' (Prédal 2002: 99). Yet Audiard's relationship with realism proves rather more complicated than a straightforward opposition – his films may appear realist in style, subject matter and *mise en scène* yet, as I will argue, this realism is infused with its own contestation; elements of his films serving to question its function as a dominant representational mode and universal model of perception.

Contesting realism: *Regarde les hommes tomber*

Audiard's first feature film remains little known outside France despite winning the Prix Georges Sadoul in 1994 and the César for best first film in 1995. The film establishes a pattern that continues in Audiard's films to date in that, despite his background and experience in scriptwriting, he has chosen to adapt existing texts and, in the case of his latest film, other films. Such decisions and working practice can be seen to mirror the central tensions between filiation and (re) invention that permeate his work. *Regarde les hommes tomber* is an adaptation of Teri White's noirish thriller *Triangle*.

With exceptional central performances from Trintignant, Kassovitz and Yanne and striking use of shooting at night, natural light and direct sound the film has a complex narrative structure that involves the gradual, halting convergence of two apparently separate story lines. In one, Simon Hirsch (Jean Yanne), a disillusioned, middle-aged travelling salesman, has struck up an unlikely friendship with a charismatic yet brutal cop, Mickey (Yvon Back). Having acted as helpless lookout in a doomed stakeout in which Mickey is shot and left in a coma, Hirsch's guilt over his lack of intervention and his frustration at the apparent indifference of the police's own investigations drive him to attempt to trace the killer himself. The second storyline introduces us to Marx (Trintignant) and Frédéric (later serially renamed as Freddy and then Johnny) (Kassovitz), an archetypal odd couple whose relationship becomes an ambiguous play of dependence and denial, shifting as often as they move on around anonymous parts of northern France before ending in Paris. Freddy's initial shyness, naivety and inarticulateness are banished as he gains confidence and power through paid work and, more notably, through assisting Marx in his trade of card tricks, violence and ultimately assassinations. Johnny's newfound identity,[1] confidence and sharp suit recall the brief glimpse afforded the audience of Mickey in his prime and reinforces the notion of potential substitution. Marx's position in the relationship mutates differently as his inability to repay debts, his growing awareness of ageing and consequent loss of nerve make him increasingly reliant on Freddy for financial and physical survival. It is 'Johnny' and Marx who killed Mickey and, on finding the pair, Hirsch kills Marx and 'adopts' Johnny.

The central protagonists are infused with a sense of temporal instability and marginal spaces common to many French films of the

---

1 The name chosen perhaps in self-conscious homage to de Niro's character in *Mean Streets* (Scorcese, 1973).

1990s[2] in which, as Martine Beugnet asserts, 'marginalité et esprit de contestation se caractérisent par un trait récurrent: ils tendent à s'exprimer par un déplacement voulu ou imposé'[3] (Beugnet 2000: 49). Both Hirsch as itinerant salesman, and Marx and Johnny as conmen, and later assassins, live emphatically nomadic existences. The parallels between them are further heightened by the emphasis on the repeated performance of their activities – Marx's card tricks to gullible audiences, Hirsch's sales patter to numerous clients.[4] Such temporal and spatial dislocation, reinforced by the repeated lack of causal development or closure in individual sequences, serves to disrupt further generic conventions and undermine identification (our first encounter with Marx and Freddy is preceded by inter-titles announcing them vaguely as 'the two others – ages before that'). The central characters are marginal in their relation to dominant social structures; Marx and Johnny are archetypal misfits, while Hirsch becomes resolutely disengaged from the familial and the social. The film's open ending rejects social normalisation or recuperation as narrative closure. Marx and Johnny are the first of a series of loners and outsiders that dominate Audiard's films and his description of them as Beckettian characters (Vachaud 1994: 38) reinforces a sense of destructive, mutual dependency but not of change.[5] While they can be likened through generic templates to Gabin and Dary in Becker's 1953 *Touchez pas au grisbi* (Herpe 1994: 34) and recall the central couples of *My Own Private Idaho* (Van Sant, 1991) or even *Bonnie and Clyde* (Siegel, 1967), such parallels remain superficial and, since the characters mutate (from salesman to avenging angel, from comic fool to assassin), they indeed contest the viability of such models, revealing 'l'impossibilité de rendre les archétypes à leurs certitudes'[6] (Herpe 1994: 34).

The film is marked overall by its combination of filmic techniques

2 Comparable marginal trajectories include *J'ai pas sommeil* (Denis, 1994) and *La Vie rêvée des anges* (Zonca, 1998).
3 'marginality and contestatory spirit ... are often articulated by displacement, whether voluntary or imposed'.
4 Hirsch's trade – selling 'cartes de visite' in order to communicate changes of identity – is deeply ironic, a banal commodification in contrast to his own disturbing transformation.
5 Audiard indeed chose Kassovitz for his 'odd mixture of juvenile idiot and malice' (Vachaud 1994: 38).
6 'the impossibility of giving archetypal figures their certitude'.

associated with realism, constructions of authenticity and immediacy (hand-held camera, direct sound, natural lighting) and their disruption through the suggestion of primal mythical narrative structures and the foregrounding of intertextual references. The film employs the generic conventions of the road movie and the *polar* to establish audience expectations which are not met. The journeys undertaken by all three central protagonists are non-linear, provide no clear temporal or spatial demarcations and, although Marx and Johnny's relationship does evolve, theirs is a journey of self-invention rather than self-discovery. Audiard asserts: 'Parce que le film de genre où on fait circuler des durs, gicler l'hémoglobine et "Fuck you man!" ne m'intéresse pas du tout. La force d'un film comme *Reservoir Dogs*, c'est avant tout la force de son scénario'[7] (Vachaud 1994: 36). Indeed its theatricality is what attracted Audiard to White's novel (Herpe 1994: 34) and bears witness to his admiration for the differently theatrical films of David Lynch[8] and David Mamet. An emphasis on theatricality, on *mise en scène* and script, is echoed in his rejection of the 'return of the real' that has featured as a major trend in French cinema since the late 1990s. Indeed, when asked to comment on contemporary French filmmakers Audiard claims not to understand their 'refusal of fiction' (Vachaud 1994: 37) and asserts, 'J'ai horreur du langage naturel dans les films. J'aime que ça parle étrange'[9] (Vachaud 1994: 36). Such strangeness is not here confined to dialogue, as the film is punctuated by elements that defamiliarise the realist settings and encourage us to look beyond the codes of filmic genre to literary and mythical narrative models.

The complex structure of *Regarde les hommes tomber*, presents the two stories in alternating sequences, yet this does not establish the classic thriller model of parallel development, but leads rather to an overriding impression of discord and disconnection between the two worlds in which they operate. This temporal layering creates the oneiric tone of *Regarde les hommes tomber*, a tone reinforced by the voice-off narration which, together with the inter-titles, works to

---

7 'I have no interest at all in the genre film in which you bring out the hard men, spray around some haemoglobin and some "Fuck you man!". The force of a film like *Reservoir Dogs* is above all the force of its script'.

8 Audiard paraphrases Lynch when expressing the motivation behind his filmmaking: 'To create a universe and see if it works' (Vachaud 1994: 37).

9 'I hate the use of natural language in films. I like them to speak strangely'.

foreground fictional construction while also evoking the dominant narrative modes of *film noir*. While it is suggested that this is the voice of Hirsch's wife, whom we meet fleetingly within the narrative, its ghostly tone and predictive, omniscient analysis remain strikingly otherworldly. Hirsch is transformed into a creature of classic night-mare; identified as a vampiric ogre who will stop at nothing (neither torture nor murder) to replace Mickey, the ambiguously desired surro-gate son, with Johnny. In White's novel, Hirsch is a policeman who, in archetypal fashion, challenges the system in order to solve the crime and Audiard's rejection of such a role has important consequences. Žižek describes the detective as 'guarantor of meaning' as the process of investigation enables both narrative coherence and closure: 'The very presence of the detective guarantees in advance the transforma-tion of the lawless sequence into a lawful sequence: in other words the reestablishment of 'normality' (Žižek 1993: 58). Audiard constructs Hirsch as a sinisterly ambiguous character whose motives remain consistently unclear and whose quest becomes centred on the gratifi-cation of his own reinvention as violent avenger through the perpetu-ation of Mickey's sadistic treatment of suspects and informants alike rather than a teleological search to solve crime or even to avenge loss. Indeed, he does not want to avenge Mickey's virtual murder (by shooting Johnny) but rather enacts his revenge upon Marx by taking Johnny from him, reflecting Audiard's likening of the character to the ambiguous giant of Tournier's *The Erl King* who carries off children in an act that does not distinguish between rescue and abduction (Vachaud 1994: 37).

Hirsch's adoption of the quest, concomitant desertion of social contexts (job, marriage) and the hermetic isolation of his cramped, chaotic car interior point to archetypal models yet can be contained within codes of realism. It is, however, the isolated pixilation of his departure scene which constructs a striking marker denoting the relegation of such codes as Hirsch sheds his identity and crosses into another (filmic) world, that of the Gothic through the explicit inter-textual reference to the carriage scene in Murnau's *Nosferatu* (1922) (Vachaud 1994: 37). As such, Hirsch imposes his reductive, vengeful view on the other plot, functioning as death-driven *deus ex machina* in opposition to Marx and Johnny's opportunistic, unplanned trajec-tory. Hirsch increasingly occupies the considerable shadows and dark spaces of the film; indeed the only space in which he communicates is in the unlit coma ward, suspended as it is between life and death and carrying with it a guaranteed lack of dialogue. The importance of such realms is asserted in the torture sequence as Hirsch's replication of Mickey's techniques is framed explicitly as a performance, or as a dream: the red curtain backdrop and spotlighting evokes the *mise en scène* of a Lynchian subconscious meeting, a discomfortingly macabre set piece worthy of *Reservoir Dogs*. Hirsch's role in this marks a striking contrast to an earlier fantasy (seemingly his own) that positioned him as disengaged voyeur of his wife's sexual identity. The ambiguous nature of these sequences, suspended between realism and fantasy, is reinforced by the presence of other uncanny images including the portentous, blinkered gaze of a dog in a veterinary collar that passes seconds before Mickey is shot, the unnerving close-ups of patterned curtains that seem barely to veil another realm and of moths flying fatally towards a light. All of these images allude to a sinister world barely hidden by banal existence. These are rather more explicable, however, than the repeated shots of bright lights which punctuate early sequences, strikingly discrete in form and in their contrast to the low-lit surroundings of the coma ward.[10] They can be read as fantastical doors of perception or indeed as images of projection – inscribing the inverted presence of the camera and the artifice of the film, a pointed marker of Hirsch's loss of differentiation between perceived realities and the fictional. However, these lights defy narrative explanation and confound the spectator in the subversion of the conventional associations of light with revelation and knowledge. In an analysis of the ontological status of light in photography, Melissa Miles suggests that the presence of 'luminous excesses' serves to disavow the associations between light, truth and presence, central to conventional etymologies of photography, in order to assert light as volatile, elusive and presenting a threat to notions of documentary truth or representation (Miles 2005: 347). These shining forms could here, perhaps, be read as an assertion of the inexplicable, of the haunting of both the real and the codes of realism as delineated in the characterisation and narrative of *Regarde les hommes tomber*.

10   The opening sequence of *De battre mon coeur s'est arrêté* contains similar floating (head)lights.

Making history: *Un héros très discret*

Audiard's second film sees the continuation of his working relationship with Kassovitz and Trintignant, and proved to be a popular box-office success, also winning a César for best director and best script at
Cannes in 1996. The film is adapted from the novel of the same name
by Jean-François Deniau (1989). While continuing a narrative focus on
the power of personal fictions,[11] *Un héros très discret* presents a central
character whose post-war reinvention as a Resistance hero is explicitly emblematic of the national reinvention of *résistancialisme* (the
retrospective Gaullist construction of the image of a France united in
resistance to the Nazi occupation), a historical revisionism promoted
by successive governments which remained officially unchallenged
for many decades.[12] Contemporary interest in such issues in France
was heightened by the completion in 1993 of the seminal study *Lieux
de mémoire* (Nora 1984–93), which analyses the (re)constructions of
memories and the selective remembering of historiography, and the
then imminent trial of war criminal Maurice Papon in which histo-
rians were to be called to give evidence in court.[13]

Such questions of the representation and revisionist discourses of
conflict are assumed to relate primarily to the Second World War but
often also comment extensively on more recent conflicts (specifically
here the Algerian war), which remain more vehemently repressed in
political and cultural discourse (Lauten 1999: 59). The late 1990s saw
the release of a series of 'Vichy heritage' films, which followed on
from the heritage genre's domination of early 1990s film production
in France, yet shared more common concerns not with contemporary
representation but with Malle's controversial *Lacombe Lucien* (1974) in
its portrayal of decisions based on personal contacts and opportunism
rather than moral certainties, and in a narrative propelled by individual
not collective will. Indeed Audiard's narrative in *Un héros très discret*,
with its playful and political interrogations of the construction of (hi)
stories, can be seen to reflect on the heritage film and cultural industries revealing 'how heritage is a postmodern spectacle which uses
history to relocate the individual subject'(Powrie 1999: 8).

11 This is reinforced by the happy use of *histoire* in French for both 'story' and
  'history'.
12 For detailed debate see Rousso (1991).
13 For detailed comparative analysis of Dehousse and Papon see Seal (2001: 109).

After a childhood sheltered in fantasy and the avoidance of war afforded the only son of a widow, Albert Dehousse (played by Kassovitz in his youth, by Trintignant as older interviewee) flees to Paris when faced with the difficult realities of accusations of collaboration against his mother and the revelation of his wife's Resistance activities. Jobless and penniless, Dehousse is befriended by the enigmatic 'Captain' who persuades him that fabrication is the only possible response to the post-war social climate. Dehousse decides to reinvent himself as Resistance hero and through rehearsal, research and a 'strategy of infiltration' passes himself off as a member of a Resistance network reunion. He is accepted, given a ministry appointment and sent to Baden-Baden as a civilian officer to manage the occupation. His strategies of reinvention are disturbed by his unexpected return to the status of outsider and the real consequences of his rank (the decision to execute deserters), he admits his imposture to his second wife and is finally tried, not for the potentially embarrassing fraud, but for bigamy.

In addition to the challenges to dominant constructions of *résistancialisme* mounted through the narrative focus on recurring patterns of opportunism, invention and denial in Dehousse's personal projections of identity and memory, the film, through its narrative and formal *mise en abyme* of documentary technique, archival authenticity and testimony, foregrounds a more general critique of the inescapably subjective and ideological nature of conventional historical discourse and (filmic) representation. The story is framed by the presence of an older Dehousse (Trintignant), who addresses the camera directly; a technique commonly used to assert the authenticity of first person testimony through proximity (close-up), voice (direct sound) and the implicit presence of an interviewer. His introduction, however, asserts the power of fiction rather than that of memory, asserting that 'la vraie vie est celle qu'on s'invente',[14] and he concludes the film with the disarming question, 'Est ce que j'ai l'air naturel?'[15] – a comment which throws doubt on the transparency of his story and provides a further *mise en abyme* of conventions of the documentary and interview footage in general. Further subversions are found in the insertion of interviews with those who profess to have known Dehousse, which interrupt the linear development of the narrative. These interviews adopt the visual and discursive codes of documen-

14 'real life is the one that you make up'.
15 'Do I come across as natural?'

tary testimony and thus recall the politically controversial formal strategies of *Le Chagrin et la pitié* (Ophüls, 1970),[16] yet their contradictory content, revealed as subjective and unreliable, recalls equally that iconic fictional narrative of personal enigma and reinvention, *Citizen Kane* (Wells, 1941).[17] The intercutting of actual footage from the period would normally function to give authenticity to the events portrayed within the main narrative of the film. Here, however, the representation of Dehousse's opportunistic self-inclusion in newsreel footage and consequent entrance into documentary evidence, challenges the boundaries between fiction and non-fiction and questions the status of the historical archive itself.

While the role of fiction may be seen to reveal the historical discourses discussed above as constructed, subjective and fallible, Audiard is careful also to stress the centrality of fiction and invention to all (cultural) discourses of identity. The film is dedicated to Pascal Ortega and can be seen as a partial response to his war drama *L'Amour fugitif* (1982) in which two deserters leave the trenches of 1917 to embark upon a personal, utopian adventure. *Un héros très discret* contains the same affirmation of the victory of imagination over the horrors of war. Dehousse's vivid imagination is stressed from the start as he sees his dead father leering at him from his portrait and spends his solitary childhood immersed in reading and role play. However, as he gets older and is reduced to copying material from the novels of others to woo his future wife, his own life becomes his greatest fiction. Dehousse's infiltration of Resistance reunions depends upon his convincing dramatic adaptation of facts and anecdotes – these stories become shared myths and those in the group become rapidly dependent upon his performance for a sense of their own potentially fragile (hi)stories. The performative nature of this identity is further foregrounded as he rehearses lines before a mirror and selects props like an actor in his dressing room, indeed his final admission to his wife concludes with the theatrical phrase: 'it's finished, curtain'.

The film's realist elements are balanced by elements that reinforce the exclusive thematic and filmic focus on the creative artifice of Dehousse's identity and form a suggestive parallel as they subvert the dominant reality effects to present a more reflexive mode which

16 Ophüls' masterpiece was given only restricted cinema release in France and was not shown on French television until 1981.
17 For further discussion of this comparison see Garbarz (1996: 16).

comments on the mimetic codes of realism itself. The use of extreme close-ups of Dehousse and camera movements that repeatedly encircle the main protagonists articulate a sense of enclosed fantasy and inscrutability while also serving to remind the spectator of the presence of the independent camera. Further elements of cinematic artifice are foregrounded as, when the key points in Dehousse's self-reinvention are accompanied by the swelling strings of a chamber orchestra, the musicians are not only heard but seen (in close-up against a black backdrop) thus disrupting their status as unmotivated musical accompaniment and inviting the spectator to consider questions of composition, labour, production and collaboration. The function of the filmic is also questioned as the temporal ellipsis of Dehousse's teenage years is represented by an accelerated sequence that evokes the early photographic iconography of Muybridge's motion studies. This invokes the scientific applications of film while suggesting that it is better suited to capturing flights of fantasy rather than the mechanical movements of physiology. On his wedding night Dehousse frames the image of Yvette's body with his hands both creating a distance of deliberate composition between himself and sensual experience and providing an explicit model of the cinematic frame.

Seeing and knowing: *Sur mes lèvres*

A concern with personal reinvention and the reflexive representation of the structures of cinema are extended in Audiard's next film, *Sur mes lèvres*. Audiard continued to contest the conventional construct of the *auteur* by choosing a different generic frame, that of an inventive thriller, but one which can contain another pairing of social outcasts. The film built on Audiard's previous success,[18] winning Césars for best sound, script and best actress for Devos (a considerable victory over Audrey Tautou's role as the eponymous heroine of the biggest French film of 2001, *Amélie*).

Carla (Emmanuelle Devos) works as a secretary in a large construction company and has severely impaired hearing. Her work status is bolstered by the opportunity to appoint her own assistant and she chooses an unlikely candidate in Paul (Vincent Cassel), a glowering,

18 A success reflected in Paramount's purchase of its remake rights in 2002 – no version is as yet in production.

unqualified, homeless ex-con. She covers for his lack of experience and expertise and so blackmails him into exacting revenge on her dishonest, misogynistic colleagues by stealing essential paperwork. Paul is forced to take on work in a nightclub to pay off a debt to a known criminal, and involves Carla in a plan to steal his cash from a recent robbery, which she undertakes by lip-reading their plans. After a suspenseful escalation of narrative complexity and violence, Carla saves Paul's life and secures the loot by successfully lip-reading his instructions.

Representations of the workplace, from the politically explicit discourse of *Ressources humaines* (Cantet, 1999) to the reductive comedy of *Le Placard* (Weber, 2001) re-emerged in French cinema of the late 1990s. *Sur mes lèvres* provides a frank portrayal of the everyday misogyny and hierarchical obsessions of the working environment, yet does not invoke the impact of the wider economic structures at play on the individual. Indeed a central function of the apparent realism of the first part of the film is to bolster the suspension of our disbelief in the second. The exclusions suffered by the central protagonists are embedded in social practices as Audiard comments: 'From the first I wanted to tell a story of two people on the margins ... to describe two forms of exclusion – people of limited talent who meet and create a "complementarity", the incompetence of one becoming the competence of the other ... I thought of deafness and matched it with lawlessness' (Lennon 2005: 23). The shifting power relationships of the central pairing in *Regarde les hommes tomber* is here expanded to cover the two worlds of office politics and the heist and is infused with a less ambiguous, sublimated sexual tension which, despite the complexities of the plot, provides the main focus for suspense: 'on avait envie d'en mettre beaucoup, de charger jusqu'à la gueule, un peu comme les structures denses de Mamet, à la limite du compréhensible, avec plein de rebondissements, pour aboutir à la seule question importante: "Vont-ils s'étreindre?" J'adorais cette ironie, que le seul véritable suspense se situe là. C'est un message plutôt optimiste, qui renvoie à une vision de l'amour courtois, où l'on tire sur la bride du désir au maximum"[19] (Rouyer and Vassé 2005: 21). Generic codes are

19 'we wanted to put lots in, to fill it right up, a little like the dense structures of Mamet, to the limits of what can be understood, with lots of twists and turns, in order to get to the single important question: "Will they embrace?" I loved this irony, that this was the only real suspense. It's a rather optimistic message, which evokes the image of courtly love, where desire is kept on the tightest rein possible'.

thus employed to construct sufficient plausibility for the spectator only to be subverted as the ultimately incidental possession of the loot acts as a catalyst for the closure of the romance plot.

Sexual tension is articulated in the film through the evolution in the framing of the central couple – their increasing physical proximity to each other stressed by the tight framing and use of close-up but also by the foregrounding of the sensual which disrupts the plot-driven dynamic of the thriller elements. The primary example of the privileging of the sensual is the reinforcement of the conventional construction of cinematic point of view by the use of subjective sound as it repeatedly replicates Carla's hearing, becoming muffled or silent. This indeed represents one of the 'rare instances of narrative cinema in which the cultural hegemony of vision is overthrown' (Sobchack 2004: 64), but arguably goes further than this in questioning the generic and broader cinematic status of the visual. The plot is driven by Carla's privileged access to information through lip-reading, a skill which is dependent upon the visual but one from which most of the audience (alongside Paul as proto-spectator and watchman in the club) is excluded. Here, seeing is no longer knowing. Thematic focus and *dénouement* coincide as Carla locates the loot, not as a result of what she has seen, but by retracing the sounds she has heard. The recurring partial obscuring of the edges of the frame (often accompanied by silence) represents the subjective sensual focus as a synaesthetic replication of Carla's particular relationship with her environment and an indication of the sensual focus of the frame, which refers to the couple's sublimated desire and not the intricacies of the heist.

The visual is inherently associated in conventional cinematic practice with structures of voyeurism, and these too are heavily implicated in the narrative through the binoculars of Carla's rooftop vigil and her spying from the chosen hiding place of the bedroom wardrobe.[20] The power imbalance upon which the (spectatorial) pleasure of voyeurism depends is challenged as the successful denouement relies on Paul's awareness that Carla is watching the apartment and on her lip-reading his direct instructions. Such spectatorial privileges are also challenged in sequences in which we see Carla express

20 The relative paucity of central female roles such as Carla's in Audiard's oeuvre is partly reinforced by his choice of generic frameworks. It is interesting, however, that the film engages with structures of voyeurism through the sensual perception of a woman (conventionally the target object of the voyeuristic gaze).

a sensuality that contrasts sharply with her office-bound existence. A series of sequences in which she models first red stilettos, Paul's shirt and new clubbing gear in front of a mirror before caressing her otherwise naked body occupy an ambiguous position in the narrative. In contrast to the tightly plotted story, the temporal and spatial disconnection (there is no red backdrop in the drab surroundings of her apartment) of these sequences is disturbing. Given the interrogation of voyeurism present in the rest of the film, an uncomfortable spectator may ask who is being positioned as the origin of these projected fantasies.

Filiations: *De battre mon coeur s'est arrêté*

The mutual reinvention of the central couple, Paul and Carla, and the romantic redemption of the final sequence foreshadow the narrative and filmic preoccupations of Audiard's latest and most commercially successful film to date, *De battre mon coeur s'est arrêté*. In addition to the increased proximity of the worlds of property development and criminality, we find a continued focus on generic mutation and the portrayal of an apparently realist *mise en scène* with a narrative that mounts a challenge to realist expectations.[21] The central protagonist struggles to forge a new identity, not in the face of social exclusion but against the familial and cultural discourses of patriarchal filiation. This is evident from the very beginning of the film through the extraordinarily poetic title that originates from a Jacques Dutronc song, *La Fille du père Noël*, which performs an exaggerated microcosm of filial determinacy.[22] The film, a gangster plot combined with an intense and sensual narrative of intitiation, is based on Toback's *Fingers* (1978), although Audiard has rejected the term 'remake' on the grounds that it represents a predominantly commercial formulation and prefers to speak instead in terms of exchanges between directors.[23]

The film presents the most explicit treatment of a central thematic

21 This is mounted here by the unlikely chance of Tom becoming a concert pianist at twenty-eight and the explicit Oedipal elements of the narrative.
22 Written in 1966, the song stages an encounter between Father Christmas's daughter and the son of the bogeyman (le Père Fouettard), revealing an (unrealised) capacity for love between those rigidly defined by the diametrical opposition of their fathers' identities.
23 Audiard, interview included in DVD release of *De battre mon coeur s'est arrêté*.

and formal focus that underlies Audiard's oeuvre to date: that of filiation. Filiation clearly persists, across national and historical borders, as a central theme of cultural practice and remains unsurprisingly evident across cinematic periods and genres from Renoir to Tim Burton. Examples of its treatment in contemporary French cinema range from dominant representations of the problematic legacy of an absent father (see *L'Histoire ancienne* (Miret, 2000) or *Le Pornographe* (Bonello, 2000)) to the metaphoric function of filiatory obsession in the context of (post)colonial history and scientific progress (*L'Intrus* (Denis, 2005)). A persistent engagement with the theme of filiation, or rather the contestation of established filial bonds, provides an auteurist trope that can be traced back through Audiard's films. *Regarde les hommes tomber* contains fake fathers, real fathers who reject their children and central characters whose apparent paternalism reveals erotic and sadistic subtexts (when Hirsch kills Marx and 'adopts' Johnny it is not the paternalistic rescue of a corrupted innocent but an act of melodramatic possession). In *Un héros très discret*, Dehousse denies filiation with either absent, slandered father or shamed mother to follow in the steps of the ambiguous father figure of the Captain and construct both new identity and family structure through the Resistance network. This is in contrast to many conventional heritage films in which the family is seen as a refuge in the face of change, transgression or otherness. *Sur mes lèvres* is exceptional, within Audiard's oeuvre, in its lack of father figures (Paul's troubled parole officer representing the only dysfunctional possibility), yet the patriarchal hierarchies of both workplace and criminal milieu reflect such models. Audiard's next production, *Les Disparus*, features the desperate search of a mother and father to reclaim their respective children. It is notable that *Fingers* does not foreground notions of filiation (the father is supportive of the son's musical career, the mother is institutionalised and her musical past unstressed), but focuses rather on a crisis of masculinity as identified with sexual performance and articulated through reductive mappings of race and hyper-virility.

De battre mon coeur s'est arrêté is infused with a sense of energy and immediacy constructed by the concentrated vitality of Duris's performance coupled with the dominance of the cinematic point of view of this central protagonist.[24] The insistence on *plans séquences*

24 Critics likened Duris to the young Delon but his performance, appearance and movement here point rather to de Niro.

and the use of handheld camera (35mm not digital video), naturalistic lighting and tight framing construct a cinematic universe which
foregrounds the tension between Tom's environment and his desires.
Following the death of his mother (an acclaimed concert pianist),
Tom (Romain Duris) has followed his father (Niels Arestrup) into
the contemporary brutality of Parisian property development. His
activities, including the barely legal trade of tracts of real estate and
the terrorising of their inconvenient inhabitants, are as brutal and
dehumanising as that of the New York mob in *Fingers*.[25] His world
is shaken by a chance encounter with his mother's former agent
who invites him to audition. Embarking on two relationships that
remain rather schematically opposed – a passionate love affair with
a colleague's wife (Atika) and the light, calm otherworldly oasis of
piano lessons with Miao Lin (Lin Dam Pham) – he neglects work to
pursue his fantasy of reinvention. His preparations for audition are
disrupted by his unsupportive father's calls on him to beat and intimi-
date his debtors and business rivals. Tom is unable to perform at the
audition and then finds his father murdered by a rival. The coda traces
him, two years later, working as Miao Lin's agent while also claiming
violent revenge, by beating the man who had his father killed, before
attending her concert.

The primary cultural model invoked here is that of a male paradigm:
the rigidly patriarchal filiation that supports Freudian discourses of
the Oedipal complex and the consequent reductive idealisation of the
mother–son relationship,[26] a relationship that is represented in the
cultural nexus of the pre-Oedipal or Lacanian imaginary. Indeed the
question Audiard poses as central to the film perpetuates this model:
'Is there an existential determinism which means one is programmed
to become the product of one's father, or can one change one's life
and how often?'(Bear 2005). Audiard's films are indeed dominated
by relationships between men, often reinforced by the conventions of
chosen generic frameworks (thriller, road movie); here, the singularly
homosocial model of the independent cinema of 1970s New York, in

---

25 The extended close-up of the sack of writhing rats provides a striking metaphor
for the brokers themselves.

26 This has implications for the representation of mother-daughter relationships
there is not room to discuss here: for a detailed contextualisation see Whitford
(1992: 262–6). It should be noted, though, that daughters are significantly
absent from Audiard's films.

which the function of female characters remains clearly defined as either objects of desire or signifiers of an idealised maternal. Father–son relationships and the wider constructs of filiation are very clearly at the heart of this film and are spelt out in an intimate, low-lit, pre-generic sequence in which Tom's colleague describes the evolution of his relationship with his father, from alienated youth through uncomfortable sexual confidant to carer and parent figure: 'C'est un moment très particulier pour les hommes, celui où décline la figure paternelle, dépositaire de l'image virile, de l'autorité, de la capacité de décision ... les garçons ont du mal à le vivre pour d'innombrables raisons, la prise de responsabilités, l'effondrement d'une illusion, d'une image paternelle forte et stable, d'un guide' (Rigoulet 2005: 33).[27]

The film is clearly open to interpretation informed by a classical Oedipal reading of the narrative. Oppositions between maternal and paternal realms remain schematic in the film, as does the apparent opposition of art (creativity, transcendence, beauty) and business (corruption, coercion, betrayal). The father's dismissive attitude towards the dead mother and music positions him as an agent of prohibition and he is associated with death through the moribund space of his apartment. Tom's indirect responsibility for his father's violent death (as revenge for the seduction of Minskov's girlfriend) constitutes a virtual parricide. This reading of the narrative is further supported by the filmic details of the text. The association of music with the maternal evokes the Lacanian imaginary – the pre-Oedipal realm of symbiotic fusion with the mother associated with the pre-linguistic. Tom's immersion in music is constant, from the escapism of his hermetic headphones (which replicate the subjective sound in *Sur mes lèvres*) and the silent practising of his piece in incongruous surroundings, to his apartment in which he engineers the coexistence of his mother's recordings and his own playing (a recording instrument even replicating a cardiograph of potential new life). The conceit of music as pre-linguistic mode is reinforced in the early lessons with Miao Lin as the only common language they initially possess is that of Bach, gesture and musical notation.[28] Tom emerges

27 'It's a very specific moment for men, as the father figure – depositary of images of virility, authority, decisiveness – is in decline ... boys find this hard to deal with for numerous reasons, the taking on of responsibilities, the fading of an illusion, of a strong, stable paternal image, of a guide'.

28 This can also be construed as a therapy session in which Tom cannot play unless Miao-Lin is positioned to avoid eye contact with her 'patient'.

from his failed immersion in the pre-Oedipal through the symbolic castration of his failed audition with M. Fox who functions here as idealised, paternal alternative. The primary narcissistic fetish of the phallus and the subsequent threat of castration are displaced here onto the pianist's hands as witnessed through the uncanny footage of a late great pianist. The fetishism is emphasised by the device of the television screen, providing the framing within the frame of the disembodied hands which recall the fingers, not of the dead mother, but of the icon of the undead, Nosferatu, and contrast greatly with Tom's hands which are represented as viscerally immersed in desire and violence. Indeed the last shot of the film focuses on Tom's bloody hands which he nurses while listening to Miao Lin play. Following the castration of unsuccessful audition, Tom seeks refuge in the paternal only to discover the actualisation of the underlying threat of the Oedipal complex: the death of his father which leaves him free to reinvent a non-oppositional dynamic between the maternal and paternal models of filiation in his role as Miao Lin's agent. Although there remains a lingering sense of loss in the redemptive closure (haunted as it is by the restless energy of Duris' performance and the powerful *mise en scène* of desire in the scenes between Tom and Aline), Tom would seem to have constructed a successful synthesis between the film's opposing worlds in acting as business agent for Miao Lin. His (somewhat vicarious) filiation with the maternal is retained as he checks the piano in the concert hall and then, contained within the same cinematic codes, he attempts to broker deals with record companies. His resultant freedom is reinforced by his choosing not to murder Minskov and thus finally sever any filiation with the criminality associated in the film with the realm of the father.[29]

Filiation and the *auteur*

Many of the central arguments contained in this chapter can be read as supporting a conventional auteurist approach to Audiard's work, yet they join with this volume and the series in which it appears in challenging such narrowly defined parameters. It remains important,

29 This is in pointed contrast to the final scenes of Toback's *Fingers*, as Jimmy's murder of his father's killer reduces him to a broken figure, last seen cowering naked beneath his piano.

therefore, to engage with such structures of interpretation, indeed there is much in Audiard's work itself that contests such models. The construction of the *auteur* reveals a clear tension in its dependence on discourses of uniqueness and originality which are placed, paradoxically, alongside anxieties of influence that continually position and reposition those directors labelled as *auteurs* within superficial auteurist genealogies which, on closer inspection, rely upon the maintenance of the very national, critical and generic boundaries that auteurism purports to transcend. Whereas auteurist tradition opposes the adaptation of literary texts to the director as scriptwriter, Audiard undertakes both activities in his filmmaking, insisting upon the inextricable links between model and reinvention. Auteurism is commonly regarded as transcending genre cinema, yet Audiard's films foreground the necessity of reflexive generic convention to his playful mutations of genre. While the *auteurs* of contemporary French cinema and the 'new new wave' are associated overwhelmingly with the discourses of realism, Audiard's films point, in consistent filmic reflexivity, to the frailty of such codes.

While a focus on the recurring engagement with questions around filiation in Audiard's oeuvre is clearly important to the construction of his traditional auteurist pedigree, they must be considered as equally central to a consideration of new constructions of auteurism, which configure the *auteur* as combining personal narrative, filmic and intertextual trajectories with essential mappings of the cultural discourses of the moment of production and reception of these works. The hierarchical and authoritarian assumptions that structure traditions of auteurism also position it as projecting an inherent political disengagement. In an important article which examines current definitions of the political in film, Jean-Michel Frodon bemoans the lack of cinematic representations of social community and asserts that 'la dévalorisation des autres formes de groupe a fait de la *cellule familiale* le principal, sinon l'unique type de collectivité utilisable dans une fiction' (Frodon 2005: 74).[30] He goes on to specify the dominant familial links of contemporary fiction film as consisting of: 'La famille, mais plus precisément les rapports de filiation, les relations parents–enfants – pas de frères et de soeurs au centre de ces histoires, très

---

30 'the devaluation of other forms of groupings has made the *family unit* the main, if not the only type of collectivity that can be used in fiction'.

peu de couples' (Frodon 2005: 74).[31] Frodon perceives such domination as a negative phenomenon with far-reaching political implications, aligning it with a privileging of: 'la tradition, l'enracinement, la
terre d'où l'on vient (et qui ne ment pas), toutes les valeurs du conser-
vatisme ou de la réaction, tout cela est encore second par rapport à
ce déni central de la politique comme capacité *d'inventer* – dans la
construction du commun aussi bien que dans sa mise en crise – des
manières d'être au monde' (Frodon 2005: 74).[32] It is to this 'capacity
to invent' that we must return here. Audiard's fiction does indeed
centre on filiation, but with the crucial difference that his narratives
do not support such structures, rather his films reveal the crushing,
reductive power they possess before staging a consistent challenge to
suffocating and predetermined models of filial relations. His central
characters remain hungry for reinvention as they struggle to break
free from their personal and allegorical filiations in order to forge
new identities based on the expression of their own desires and new
collaborative models. Such focus on the process and power of reinvention echoes a more radical Deleuzian model of change and identity. In
a text that begins with the discussion of Oedipal trajectories in film,
Deleuze suggests different strategies for representing evolution and
change: 'becoming produces nothing by filiation: all filiation is imaginary. Becoming ... concerns alliance ... not hereditary, but communicative or contagious' (Deleuze and Guattari 1988: 238).

Perhaps such strategies can be extended as indicative of the
emergence of a new construction of the *auteur*: one which foregrounds
the *auteur* as nexus of communicative (even contagious) alliances.
Audiard's films, which delight in unpicking the threads of personal,
generic and filmic identity (from myths of French national cultural
memory to reductive paradigms of patriarchal filiation), in playing
with established expectations of spectatorial identification and narrative closure and in revealing the empowering implausibility of (such)
archetypal cinematic figures, provide an ongoing exploration of such
possibilities.

31 'The family, but more precisely those linked through filiation, parent–child
   relations – there are no brothers and sisters at the heart of these stories and very
   few couples'.
32 'tradition, rootedness, your country of origin (which never lies), all these
   conservative and reactionary values are secondary in relation to the central
   denial of the political (in the construction of community as well as its location
   in crisis) as the capacity *to invent* ways of being in the world'.

References

Baudry, Claude (2005), 'Audiard, le fils', www.artsetspectacles.nouvelobs.com/cinema2105–086.html, accessed 10/10/2005.

Bear, Liza (2005), 'Reworking Toback's "Fingers": Jacques Audiard on "The Beat That My Heart Skipped"', www.indiewire.com/people-050701audiard.hml, accessed 23/10/2005.

Beugnet, Martine (2000), *Marginalité, sexualité, contrôle dans le cinéma français contemporain*, Paris, L'Harmattan.

Deleuze, Gilles and Guattari, Félix (1988), 'Becoming-intense, becoming-animal, becoming-imperceptible', in *A Thousand Plateaus. Capitalism and Schizophrenia*, London, Athlone Press.

Frodon, Jean-Michel (2005), 'Famille politique', *Cahiers du cinéma* (September), 72–6, 74.

Garbarz (1996), 'Un héros très discret', *Positif*, 423, 16–17.

Herpe, Noël (1994), 'Regarde les hommes tomber: le verbe en quête de chair', *Positif*, 403, 34–5.

Lauten, Kathryn M. (1999), '"Dusting off" Dehousse: *Un héros très discret*' (Audiard, 1996), in P. Powrie (ed.), *French Cinema in the 1990s: Continuity and Difference*, Oxford, Oxford University Press, pp. 58–68.

Lennon, Peter (2005), 'All that glisters...', *The Guardian* (25 May), 23.

Miles, Melissa (2005), 'The burning mirror: photography in an ambivalent light', *Journal of Visual Culture*, 4 (3), 329–49.

Nora, Pierre (1984–93), *Lieux de mémoire (Realms of Memory)*, Paris, Gallimard.

Powrie, Phil (1999), 'Introduction', in Powrie (ed.), *French Cinema in the 1990s: Continuity and Difference*, Oxford, Oxford University Press, pp. 1–24.

Prédal, René (2002), *Le Jeune cinéma français*, Paris, Nathan.

Rigoulet, Laurent (2005), 'Cinéaste à reculons', *Télérama*, 2879 (19 March), 33–4.

Rousso, H. (1991), *The Vichy Syndrome: History and Memory in France since 1944*, Boston, Harvard University Press.

Rouyer, Philippe and Vassé, Claire (2005), 'Entretien avec Jacques Audiard', *Positif*, 529, 21–5, 21.

Seal, Howard (2001), 'Screening the past; representing resistance in *Un héros très discret*', in L. Mazdon (ed.), *France on Film*, London, Wallflower, pp. 107–18.

Sobchack, Vivian (2004), *Carnal Thoughts: Embodiment and Moving Image Culture*, Berkeley, University of California Press.

Vachaud, L. (1994), 'Entretien avec Jacques Audiard. Du côté du cinéma', *Positif*, 403, 36–40.

Whitford, M. (1992), 'Mother–daughter relationships', in E. Wright (ed.), *Feminism and Psychoanalysis: A Critical Dictionary*, Oxford, Blackwell, pp. 262–6.

Žižek, Slavoj (1993), *Looking Awry: An Introduction to Lacan Through Popular Culture*, Cambridge, MA, and London, MIT.

3

Ethics in the ruin of politics: the Dardenne brothers

Martin O'Shaughnessy

The Dardenne brothers first achieved major critical recognition with *La Promesse* (1996) and have confirmed their status as leading international filmmakers by twice winning the Cannes *Palme d'Or*, the first time with *Rosetta* (1999), the second with *L'Enfant* (*The Child*, 2005). Coming between the latter two films, *Le Fils* (*The Son*, 2002) was also a striking critical success. The four films manifest the kind of thematic, stylistic and, indeed, spatial unity that one might typically associate with the figure of the cinematic *auteur*. At a thematic level, all figure a social implosion that is translated through dysfunctional families and through the incapacity of one generation to pass on anything positive to the next. All revolve in one way or another around murder and the sense that we now live in a world where non-recognition or outright destruction of the other has become the norm.[1] Stylistically, while there is a clear radicalisation between *La Promesse* and *Rosetta*, the brothers' films have consistent recourse to the same rawness, to the same close, unrelenting tracking of their minimal cast of characters as the tension between fundamental ethical choices is played out, not primarily in words, but across their bodies. At the spatial level, the films always return faithfully to the brothers' hometown of Seraing, in Belgium, an old working-class heartland now in the throes of de-industrialisation. These thematic, stylistic and spatial resemblances might suggest that the Dardenne brothers had produced a uniquely coherent oeuvre, a model of auteurist consistency. Yet, the brothers' filmmaking career

---

1 *L'Enfant* revolves around a father who sells his own child. Not a killing in a strict physical sense, this is nonetheless an act of enormous symbolic violence to all intents and purposes equivalent to a murder.

did not begin with *La Promesse*, the film that brought them initial international recognition. Apart from making two earlier fiction films (one of which, *Je pense à vous* (1992), an important transitional work, will be discussed here), they made a number of documentaries that, although almost completely unknown outside their native Belgium, cast important light on their later trajectory.

The documentary work is worth returning to both for its intrinsic merits as creative or poetic documentary and for the way in which it provides a pre-history for the later fictions, a pre-history which not only points to the novelty of the socio-political terrain upon which they have to operate, but also helps us to understand some of the radical stylistic and formal choices that they make. The documentaries sought to explain, prolong and question a leftist tradition of struggle at a time when it and the class associated with it were entering into profound crisis. The later fictions operate in the ruins of the working class and in the absence of the politics of which they were seen as the vanguard. While the documentaries can thus profitably be put to work to explain the traumatic changes out of which the fictions emerge, it would be a mistake not to see the common drive shared by the two categories of film. This drive is best encapsulated in the word resistance.

The resistance that runs through the brothers' films can be understood in several different ways. It can be seen, firstly and most obviously, at the level of thematic content. The documentaries systematically set out to record the voices of those who had said no to the established order, be it when Belgium was under Nazi occupation or be it in the post-war period, when it seemed, for a time, as if the power of capital and of dominant social groups could be seriously threatened. Occupying a social space from which such collective resistances seem banished, the fictions figure individualised resistances.[2] Lacking a politics, these can take perverse forms, but nevertheless signal the protagonists' refusal of their circumstances and thus their recalcitrant agency in an oppressive world of which they are never simply the reflections. Resistance, secondly, is the resistance of that which is filmed. In the documentaries, this takes more obvious forms. Filming real people, revisiting historical events, the brothers have to come to terms with a raw material not of their own making,

2 On this consistent commitment to tracking resistance and on the shift from collective, political resistance to individual, moral opposition see Dardenne (2003).

which inevitably resists them. Fiction might seem able to abolish the friction of this encounter with the real by allowing the directors to invent their own infinitely pliant raw materials. Yet the brothers' films show a constant effort to build resistances into a fictional world and invented characters that are never simply available for our scrutiny but which run ahead of us or escape our gaze. Resistance, thirdly, is the brothers' own resistance to that which they show, a resistance that means that they are never simply faithful documentary makers, nor unquestioning fictional realists. Thus, while the documentaries refuse the simple erasure of a tradition of struggle, they simultaneously question the mythical stories and images at the heart of that tradition. Working in a socio-political context in which social relations seem condemned to violence and in which there seems no available language with which to name injustice, the fictions nonetheless seek to show a way out of the real that they might otherwise seem merely condemned to inhabit. They do this, and this is a central question to which we shall return, by creating ethical choices that reopen a fragile sense of alternative possibility. The multi-faceted resistance of the films calls in turn for an engaged yet resistant spectatorship, one that refuses to see from an objectifying distance but one that also avoids emotional or political absorption into that which is shown.

The documentaries

Made at a historical moment – the late 1970s and early 1980s – when a durable tradition is facing catastrophic interruption, the documentaries are clearly marked by the tension between continuity and discontinuity. Together they evoke a leftist struggle that goes from anti-Nazi resistance (*Le Chant du rossignol*, 1978), through the great Belgian national strike of 1960 (*Lorsque le bateau de M. Léon descendit la Meuse pour la première fois*, 1979) and efforts to prepare for another strike that never came (*Pour que la guerre s'achève, les murs devraient s'écrouler/Le Journal*, 1980) to the work of radical playwright Jean Louvet, a writer who had founded a workers' theatre in the 1960s but who found that the cause he had been part of had unravelled (*Regarde Jonathan*, 1983).[3]

3 For a rich series of articles on the brothers' early work, from the documentary years up to *La Promesse*, see Mélon and d'Autreppe (1996–97). My special thanks go to Marc-E. Mélon for his vital help at an early stage of this research.

Continuities between the films are not only at the level of their political subject matter, but also at the level of the people shown. *Lorsque le bateau* is made with militants first contacted during the filming of *Le Chant du rossignol*, while Edmond, the leading figure in *Pour que la guerre s'achève*, can already be seen in *Lorsque le bateau*. The banks of the river Meuse and the increasingly empty factories of the old Belgian industrial heartland region are also a constant presence in the films. These ever-present locations carry with them a memory of an epic history of industrialisation and of class struggle while simultaneously testifying, through hollowed out factories and streets and squares now returned to banal, quotidian activities, to the withdrawal of that history. In the same way, while the witnesses brought forward by the film have the power to summon up past epics, their re-absorption into the everyday underlines the epics' contemporary withdrawal.

Lorsque le bateau begins by showing the Monsieur Léon of the title as he puts the finishing touches to a boat that he has built and which he will sail down the Meuse on its maiden voyage. The boat trip is put to double use. One use is metonymic and mnemonic, the other allegorical and interrogative. The first is in evidence each time a location summons up either a memory from M. Léon, a clip from archive footage of the 1960 strike, or a fellow leftist who, as if responding to the boat's horn, materialises in order to recall his or her role in past events in that place. The second use is seen when the boat, the river's banks, a solitary seagull and the sun are used to ask whether a left-wing epic has come to an end or whether the journey is still unfinished. Thus, for example, the seagull's mobility is used to evoke a still-live sense of the possible while the river's banks evoke the constraints of the real. *Pour que la guerre s'achève* engages in a similar interplay of the metonymic and the allegorical, the retrospective and the interrogative. If *Lorsque le bateau* is framed as a journey narrative, *Pour que la guerre s'achève* is told as a war, with factory walls playing Jericho to its hero, Edmond's Joshua. 'Marches' around the factory site are used to summon up memories of past campaigns while also underlining their absence from a present reclaimed by pacified routines. The largely empty site suggests a battle that has not so much been won or lost but whose terrain has been evacuated leaving one side not knowing what to do. A solitary cat found in the ruins is used to evoke the absence of the working class as epic, collective protagonist. Finally, Edmond's chess set is used to summarise a battle in which the militants were originally able to hold their own but have now lost most of their pieces, with the remainder scattered. As in *Lorsque le bateau*, the complex interplay of heroic past and unheroic present, of archive footage of struggle and images of isolated and solitary militants both preserves a memory of struggle and keeps leftist mythology at a distance. Symptomatic of the films' resistance of their materials, of their refusal to be absorbed by stories with which they are clearly sympathetic, this distance is accentuated by ironic and comic contrasts between Edmond's little chess set or Léon's small boat and the grandiose historical epic that they are used to evoke. Distance opens a space in which an epic leftist grand narrative can be interrogated rather than simply celebrated. The films do not simply retell leftist histories, they question the broader frame within which these histories have traditionally made sense. It is in this way that one might see them as poetic documentaries, as films that self-consciously and sometimes playfully explore the different interpretations that might be attached to what they show.

With *Regarde Jonathan*, open-ended interrogation shifts to pessimistic summation. Louvet is a committed artist who has not so much left the struggle as been left by it and is now obliged to ask himself what he can still find to write about. The film intercuts between shots of him reading from and discussing his work, dramatised extracts from the plays, shots of dilapidated industrial landscapes and still and moving archive images. The characteristic allegorical elements are here provided by a boxer and a series of trains to which the boxer, once nicknamed *la locomotive*, also belongs. If, in his locomotive phase, he would seem to equate to the working class as motor of history in a context of class struggle, his current situation, boxing only shadows, underlines a loss of historical agency. Another train, evoked by quotation from Louvet's work, is 'le train du bon dieu',[4] an untheorised utopia whose arrival the common people await. The third train, the only one still available, in a way that underlines the absence of the other two, is the ordinary one that carries Louvet through the Belgian landscape as he asks what he, as a once committed writer, can now do. His answer is worth exploring because it casts light not simply on his evolution, but on that of the Dardenne brothers themselves.

Louvet notes first of all the loss of the totalising ideology that had

4 'the good Lord's train'.

supplied an explicit or implicit structure for his and many others' work. He notes too not simply the absence of the political people but the dissolution of the social fabric itself. He comments, 'je ne vois plus de fable possible'.[5] It has become impossible not simply to tell overarching histories but all the small stories that only made sense as part of a broader historical unfolding. A totalising leftist language has been shattered into fragments. All that remains, as an invisible pen writes on the screen, are 'des mots solitaires en attente d'histoire',[6] linguistic scraps no longer held together by a meaning-giving framework. This recognition of the loss of a language provides a negative response to the question initially put in *Lorsque le bateau*, 'Quel est le langage révolutionnaire non condamné à mort par l'histoire?'.[7] It could reasonably be objected of course that, passed down to the people from above, this language was never truly theirs, but, with its story of the autonomous self-expression of self-educated, radical workers, *Pour que la guerre s'achève* underlined how it could be appropriated from below. The title of the newspaper established by Edmond and his comrades was tellingly *La Voix du peuple* (*The Voice of the People*). Louvet suggests that the task which remains after the loss of this language, with the sense of historical possibility and of social connectivity that it expressed, is the need to 'comptabiliser ce qui nous reste d'humain'.[8] With their obsessive searching for the human in an inhuman social terrain, the Dardenne brothers' recent fictions may be seen as a realisation of this project. The ground upon which they are condemned to work is announced by Louvet on both the sociological and the symbolic levels. Socially, their cinema locates itself where the working class used to be and where social connectivity is now precisely what is lacking. Symbolically, it operates in a space where a totalising leftist language once was. Where a leftist analysis was once available to raise people above their immediate situation, the Dardenne brothers' later films show characters who are plunged into a real from which meaning has been withdrawn and with no available vantage point from which to rise above it. Meaning, to the extent that it can be rediscovered, will have to come from within the real as a product of embodied collisions. Values or a sense of justice that might

5 'I see no possibility of creating stories'.
6 'solitary words waiting for a story'.
7 'What is the revolutionary language not condemned to death by history?'
8 'calculate what humanity we retain'.

provide a vantage point from which to judge interactions will have to be rebuilt in the ruins of the old politics.

The documentaries also point to a transition in the articulation of the bodily that will be continued in the fictions. In the opening minutes of *Lorsque le bateau* the narrator's voice tells us how Léon's body had always been moved by a series of routine gestures that tied his personal, embodied history into something much broader. Thus, the gestures he learnt as an apprentice accompanied him to the blast furnaces, helped build the town, were put in the service of resistance and finally constructed the little boat that he is to sail down the Meuse. Despite this apparent continuity, something clearly changes with the building of the boat when gestures and bodily action are redirected to a purely personal project. The body is still a repository of collective memories but embodied action can now only be connected to current processes – notably the crisis of the left – allegorically. This same disconnection is seen at work in *Pour que la guerre s'achève* where Edmond's now innocuous 'marches', his house and its furnishings can only summon the memories of gestures, such as counting out newspapers, that once tied the bodily and the everyday into class struggle. Thus *Lorsque le bateau* and *Pour que la guerre s'achève* begin to announce the radical shift in the articulation of the corporeal that will make itself felt in the later films where embodied struggle, no longer part of anything beyond itself, no longer given meaning by a language or a tradition, will be condemned to brute immediacy. It is therefore no accident that relations of apprenticeship figure repeatedly in the fictions. In a world in which connectivity between generations has been broken, apprenticeship figures an embodied knowledge that can still be transmitted to the young, teaching them to engage meaningfully with the world of things and connecting them to others.

Uneasy transitions: *Je pense à vous*

Coming after the documentaries and before the well-known fictions, *Je pense à vous* is a film that the brothers have repeatedly rejected for its conventional plotting and cinematography and its recourse to established actors who drew on their own performance repertoires to create pre-formatted characters, faces and gestures. But despite its failings and relative conventionality, it is important for the light it casts on the transition of one framing of social struggle to a radically different one and for an initial sketching out of some of the core thematic concerns of the later films. It begins as a steelworker and his wife celebrate the building of the handsome detached home that would seem to mark their complete social integration. At the same time, the town, Seraing, is mobilising to protect its steelworks from closure in the face of global over-production. Commitments seem to have been obtained from the government. At a mass meeting, complete with banners, in the town square, a young girl is able to pronounce confidently 'Seraing vivra'. But, things quickly change. Closure is announced without the workers seeming able to resist. The hero, previously a self-confident skilled worker, loses his job and is condemned to unemployment. He works briefly as a nightwatchman entrusted with the monitoring of a slagheap, thus consigned, with rather obvious symbolism, to watch over the remnants of the past rather than to build the future, as he had once done. Having disappeared, he resurfaces as an unskilled labourer in the illegal economy, somewhere in the countryside, digging trenches and living in a roadside hotel that also serves as a brothel. He has effectively collapsed as a moral and a social being and is no longer part of an integrated group. In a way also characteristic of the later films, he is nonetheless offered a possibility of salvation, a way out of the fallen real in which he otherwise seems condemned to remain. This happens when the gang-master beats up a worker in front of his fellow labourers, by the caravan that serves as a mobile office. Choosing active solidarity over passive spectatorship, the hero intervenes and attacks the gang-master. The next scene finds him as he sits silently binding his fellow worker's wounded hand. Having thus reasserted his status as an ethical being (by refusing injustice and by caring for another), he is able to return to his town and his family. He finds them as they celebrate carnival. Seeing him, his son throws him an orange that he throws on to his wife, as family unity is tellingly reasserted through gesture not words.

Although unsatisfactory in several ways, *Je pense à vous* is important for how it shows a dramatic shift in the framing of social struggle, a shift that has yet to find an adequate style. The film begins by showing a context within which epic, collective struggle can draw on a tradition of group pride and solidarity and can locate itself in relation to national and international contexts, not least through the mobilisation of a shared language of resistance. In the later stages, however, resistance has become raw, local and mute. No longer situated in the historically charged locale of the steel-making town, it is shown in a place (a field) emptied of significance and marked by impermanence (the caravan). No longer able to call on shared meanings, it passes directly through bodies, as must the reconnection to others seen in the hand-binding and the passing of oranges. What was a political resistance – one mediated through collective instances – has shifted to become a predominantly ethical one arising out of a moment of individual responsibility in the face of the suffering of another.

Having accompanied a leftist politics and working-class traditions as they were dismantled, the Dardenne brothers remained contemporary of their time by moving into the space of social collapse, brute oppression and raw resistance. Yet, as they themselves note, they had not yet found an adequate style. Their content had become raw while their filmmaking, prisoner of a cinematic inheritance that, as novice fiction filmmakers, they were ill-placed to filter, was still decidedly over-cooked. This makes itself felt, for example, at the level of shot composition. In *Je pense à vous*, shots tend to be carefully framed, with leading characters coming neatly to predictable, central positions, so that an increasingly raw content sits ill with still academic framing. In a similar way, although the content suggests the rise of a new, brute corporeality, the performances remain conventional, an acting out from within of character. Finally, although showing its hero's eviction from a shared tradition and a social context, the film is both socially dense, with a cluster of supporting characters largely absent from the later films, and heavily plotted, with a developed family back story and a moving but conventional romance. The ending, with a reunited family and happy, good-looking couple in a still strong social group, confirms the failure to break sufficiently with cinematic convention and audience expectation. At the level of content, the film has shown the way to a cinema of ethical agency that might profitably occupy the ruins of an elaborated politics, but at the level of form and style the project of an ethical cinema remains incomplete.

Finding a form, refining a style

The experience of *Je pense à vous* clearly caused a rethinking of the Dardenne brothers' filmmaking practice and drove them towards the formal and stylistic choices that characterise their later films. In particular, it pushed them to pare away all those conventional elements that might prevent the underlying brutality of the contemporary order making itself felt in their work.[9] Thus, from *La Promesse* on, they have abandoned a cinema of stars, often preferring amateur and little-known performers in a drive to prevent the pre-formatted gestures and expressions of established actors blocking the entry of the real into their films (Dardenne 2005: 72). The contrast between the very glamorous and stylish Fabienne Babe in *Je pense à vous* and the made-to-be unglamorous Émilie Dequenne in *Rosetta* is a telling one. Babe's character's appearance invites a pleasure in looking confirmed by the jealousy she causes in her husband and the attraction she arouses in her brother-in-law. Dequenne's Rosetta is one that we are rather uncomfortably made to accompany.[10] Tellingly, in the one scene in *Rosetta* where seduction might have been expected, the scene where she eats and then dances with Riquet, her one friend, she is dressed in trousers rather than the skirt and tights that she wears at all other times. Visual seduction is not simply not invited, it is actively blocked. The avoidance of star performers might seem to be belied by the repeated presence of leading actor Olivier Gourmet in the later films. But Gourmet, an actor rather than a star, a powerful rather than an attractive performer, is very much at home with the Dardenne brothers' ascetic style.[11]

Asceticism also consistently makes itself felt in the *mise en scène* of the brothers' films. The décor of *La Promesse* is a largely bare one with indoor action taking place in dowdy interiors and exterior shots located in anonymous streets, sometimes with the shell of an epic, industrial landscape as mute backdrop. But rather than accumulating a series of signs of social misery, as might a realism of surface, the

9   After *Je pense à vous* and while preparing *La Promesse*, Luc Dardenne tellingly wrote in his journal: 'Sentiment d'engorgement, d'encombrement. Il faudrait balayer, déblayer, découvrir une langue plus nue' (Dardenne 2005: 42) ('A feeling of bloating, of clutter. There is a need to sweep away, to clear the ground, to find a more denuded language').

10   Dequenne is not simply an unglamorous actress. Rather, a combination of costume, lack of make-up, performance and situation is used to make her unglamorous. (Austin 2004: 257–60).

11   Jérémie Rénier, star of *La Promesse* and of *L'Enfant* might seem another exception. But Rénier, like Gourmet, is clearly happy to work along the lines laid down by the brothers and was at the time of *La Promesse* a complete unknown.

decors are above all the locations in which actions unfold, so that accompaniment of characters is again privileged over any voyeurist pleasure or horror. The stripping of visual detail is rigorously pursued in *Rosetta* and *Le Fils*. Most of the action of *Rosetta* is concentrated in a few sparse locations, notably a caravan park and a bus station. Where their presence is foregrounded, objects are never used to create a sense of atmosphere or social milieu but are there because Rosetta or other characters interact with them.[12] This paring down reaches its peak in *Le Fils* where interior locations are not only Spartan but all tend to reproduce the same cold colour scheme of blues, whites and greys. The asceticism of décor and objects is mirrored by the paring away of the cast and the simplification of character. *La Promesse* still has a range of minor characters. *Rosetta*'s cast is reduced to a handful. *Le Fils* has a core cast of two, or, if one counts the hero's ex-wife, three. One could argue that this ruthless paring down is expressive of the situation that the characters find themselves in, trapped in hostile circumstances, disconnected from the dense working-class social network still to be found in the early part of *Je pense à vous*. But it is evidence too of a desire to move away from a cinema of detached looking to one of ethical engagement. Testifying to a determination to focus not on the external signs of social misery but on underlying conflicts and tensions, it allows stark ethical choices to appear with full clarity. The asceticism of the *mise en scène* is rigorously mirrored in the paring down of the plots.

There are two compelling reasons why the Dardenne brothers' films need to lose the plot. Or, rather, there are two types of plot that need to be lost. The first plot, of the sort to be found in *Je pense à vous*, is the well-crafted plot of cinematic convention, which blocks the entry of the real into the film. The second is the plot that the characters themselves craft to survive in a world where each has become enemy of each. It is only by losing this second plot through the recognition of the other's right to exist that characters can break out of the brutal, inhuman real in which they are condemned to move and bring the films to a close.[13] Escape from the first kind of plot is

12 For a rich account of *Rosetta* as action heroine and of her interaction with objects see Burdeau (1999).

13 'Le mensonge exige beaucoup de construction. Le mal est une construction passionnée ... La vérité, le bien apparaissent alors comme une révélation. Révélation qui est délivrance de toutes les intrigues' (Dardenne 2005: 153) ('Lies

inscribed within the architecture of films that, rather than ever being linear unfoldings, are typically conflicted situations that, were it not for the restless movement of the characters, one might be tempted to call immobilised. Each situation has its own dynamic, its own set of constitutive tensions, but each is also a variant of what one might call a master situation of choice between self-preservation and recognition of the other's right to exist. Because each film expresses an essentially unvarying tension, each tends to proceed through parallels and recurrences that, never merely repetitions, bring underlying violences ever closer to the surface while driving the character ever further into a corner, until he or she loses his own plot and rediscovers his or her humanity.[14]

La Promesse or the search for fixity in a world of flows

The core dynamics of *La Promesse* are circulation and dissimulation. Its core tension is between destruction and assistance of the other. At the heart of the film are Roger, a people trafficker, and his son, Igor, an apprentice mechanic. A parasite in the de-industrialised landscape, Roger profits from the international flow of people, puts the migrants to work illegally, exploits and cheats them and betrays them to the authorities when it is expedient. By turning the flow of people into a flow of cash, he can pay for the house where he and Igor will live, thus giving them a fixed point, a shelter, in a world of flows. Yet, in a world where there are not enough homes for all, the choice of fixity for some comes at the price of enforced movement for others. While this choice goes to the heart of the contemporary order, it is not normally one that people are required to confront, so to speak, face to face. However, by placing their films at the margins, at the hard edge of exploitation,

---

need a lot of building. Evil is a passionate construction ... of which one has to show all the cogs, all the connections. The truth, good appear then as a revelation. A revelation which is a deliverance from all plots').

14 In an interview in *Cahiers du cinéma* the brothers explain how they sought to make *Rosetta* even less plot-led than the already raw *La Promesse*. They explain: 'Dans *La Promesse*, nous filmions une intrigue entre des personnages, ici nous nous sommes intéressés aux gestes. C'est plus radical dans ce sens-là, plus minimal' (Dardenne and Dardenne 1999: 47) ('In *La Promesse* we were filming a story with characters, here [in *Rosetta*] we were interested in gestures. It's more radical in that sense, more minimalist').

the Dardenne brothers are able to make the brutal consequences of general choices more visible. While the better off, those nearer the centre, can distance themselves from the consequences of action and mediate between themselves and those with whom global economic processes bring them into connection, not least through the impersonal power of money, those at the bottom are forced to come nearer to the raw ugliness of the contemporary order. This becomes rather graphically clear at the beginning of *La Promesse* when Roger is told that the sewage outlet of the house he has overfilled with migrants has become blocked. He instructs one of the house's inhabitants to put in a broader down-pipe. A profoundly corrupt character, he seeks to turn the flow of people into a flow of money without facing the flow of shit that necessarily accompanies the other flows. He holds shit at a distance, where he can, by paying others to do his dirty work and by lying as and when necessary, adding another flow, the flow of empty words, to the multiple circulations. Igor, his son, is an innocent, an adolescent who has yet to become a man. Although his apprenticeship would seem to offer him a legitimate position of fixity, a set of practices and rules that would simultaneously root him in the world of things and give him a useful place in the social order, his father repeatedly pulls him out of the garage to assist in his dealings. Repeatedly placed in movement by conflicting demands upon him, Igor is dragged into the world of flows, part victim, part exploiter, a character defined by the tension that traverses him. He is torn. When and where he can, he helps people to whom he is drawn. When he harms them, he dissimulates or seeks to place an insulating distance between himself and the harm he has done.

The film does not leave Igor in a stable situation of tension between help and harm. It forces him to a series of choices, resisting through this formal mechanism the corruption of the real that it figures. His first choice is the wrong one. Made to decide between his apprenticeship and his father, he chooses the latter, a choice of corruption over self-discipline. The second choice is more dramatic. When inspectors come unexpectedly to the house that they are using illegal migrants to construct, the migrants are made to hide. However, one, an African called Amidou, falls from the scaffolding and is hurt. He makes Igor promise to look after his wife and child. Igor puts a tourniquet on his leg. Unwilling to risk exposure as an illegal employer, Roger removes the tourniquet, effectively committing a murder to which Igor, by failing to resist, consents. Another revelatory flow, the flow of blood, now appears and has to be hidden, as is Amidou's body, which is buried in concrete at the base of the house. Characteristically, Igor tries to help Assita, Amidou's widow, and her infant, but, characteristically too, he will not tell her the truth. Resolute in her loyalty to husband and infant, a recalcitrant point of fixity in a world of flows, Assita refuses to move on. As if determined to save the mobile Igor, the film forces him to another choice when he learns that Roger appears to want to sell Assita into the international sex trade as a way to move her on. Igor finally takes the right decision, breaks with his corrupt father, escapes from his self-serving plot and rescues Assita, her child and himself as moral being. As the film ends, he is finally able to look Assita in the face and tell her the truth, thus achieving a moment of ethical stillness among the film's various flows and evasions.

In a film structured by repetition, Igor's closing confession is the third, rare instance in the film when words carry real weight and, rising above the perpetual present of the world of flows, can reconnect past and future. The first is Igor's apprenticeship, a contract between adult and adolescent whereby both are tied together in a relation of mutual obligation around the transmission of a knowledge. The second is the promise that ties Igor to the future needs of Amidou's wife and child in a way that establishes a durable interpersonal obligation. Closing the film, reversing the temporal direction of the promise, the confession re-establishes a broken bond of trust between Igor and Assita. The documentaries showed the disconnection of embodied experience from a totalising leftist language that connected self to other and past to future. *La Promesse* underlines the rarity of words that can perform such a task in a fallen contemporary order. A meaningful language that can rise above the needs of the moment can only re-emerge, it would seem, in those rare cases where a real and durable commitment can still be made between generations, between self and other.

Rosetta or drowning in matter

More radically corporeal than *La Promesse*, *Rosetta* has to make its connections without even those few meaningful words to which its predecessor retains access. The film's central dynamic is provided by the desire of its heroine, a character on the outside of society, to be on the inside.[15] Yet, in a world where inclusion is conditional upon a durable employment that is rationed, one person can be brought in only if another is expelled. Rosetta is thus caught in the tension between existing socially and the social destruction of the other that this entails. At its most brutal, this tension expresses itself in a choice between murder and suicide, acts of extreme violence that bring the latent, mediated brutality of the social order to the surface. Rosetta is a warrior, an action heroine almost constantly on the move, who lays siege to the social world to which she seems condemned not to belong.[16] In a film again patterned by recurrences, we repeatedly track her as she leaves her caravan site location on the outskirts and heads into the town where she repeatedly fails to gain a durable place. The visible displacement of one person by another is also a recurrent event. When Rosetta obtains work, she is forced to see the person that she has displaced. When she loses her job, she is able to see the person who replaces her. When she is rebuffed by the town to which she lays siege and returns to her caravan site, another series of repeated gestures is seen. These underline how, like a wartime resister, she must resort to clandestinity and live off the land: she changes from shoes to Wellington boots; she raises the wire so as to enter the site without being seen; she checks the fish trap which she illicitly places in a pond on the site. The site is a place of survival, of elemental existence where, no longer mediated by a network of social ties, brute need and human body collide. Rosetta's existence there revolves around fishing, keeping warm, eating simple food, drinking water and fetching gas. Thus plunged into matter by her need to survive, she seems to risk engulfment. The sequence where her alcoholic mother knocks her into the fishpond and leaves her floundering, trapped in the mud, is not some strange interruption of her normal state. Rather, it is a radicalisation of it, an expression of human life stripped of any humanity and reabsorbed into matter and the natural world.

It is another incident of near drowning that nonetheless begins

15 'Elle est *out*, dehors, et elle veut aller dedans, à tout prix. Ce n'est pas plus compliqué que cela' (Dardenne and Dardenne 1999: 48) ('She is outside and she wants to go inside, at any price. It's no more complicated than that').

16 'C'est un film de guerre. Rosetta va au front à la recherché d'un travail ... Seule importe la victoire: avoir un travail, trouver une place' (Dardenne 2005: 86) ('It's a war film. Rosetta goes to the front to find a job ... The only thing that matters is victory: having a job, finding a place').

Rosetta's rescue and forces the human to reappear in an inhuman order. A young man, Riquet, insists on helping her, initially by assisting in her pursuit of work. Later, while helping her recover her fish trap from the pond, he too falls in, a typical example of recurrence with variation. Rosetta knows that if he drowns she will get his job. She hesitates as a choice between solidarity and murder is played out across her body and expressed through her movements and gestures. Eventually, she runs to fetch a branch to pull him out. Later, though, she finds a less dramatic way to be rid of him by telling the boss that he is selling his own waffles from the stall. The sacked Riquet now pursues Rosetta, refusing, like Assita in *La Promesse*, to conveniently disappear. Rosetta eventually cracks and resigns her job, thus implicitly reiterating the decision, initially made when she saved Riquet, not simply to displace the other. Instead, she prepares to kill herself, thereby confirming the social erasure that ensues from abandonment of the struggle to be on the inside. Characteristically, testifying to the Dardenne brothers' unflinching commitment to their characters, the film gives her another chance. The gas runs out. Even as she falls on the way back to her caravan with a fresh canister too heavy to carry, Riquet once again arrives on the scene. The defiantly independent young woman lets herself be helped, finally admitting, again through gesture not word, that she cannot stand alone.

Like *La Promesse*, *Rosetta* uses the margins to bring out the inhuman violence at the heart of contemporary reality. Athough Rosetta seems at war with a social order that excludes her, her rebellion is conformist. She simply takes competitive individualism and its denial of interdependence and the other to their logical consequences, making their full brutality appear in a context where no financial or institutional mediations are available to hold them at a distance. As with Igor in *La Promesse*, it is only when Rosetta loses the plot and acknowledges the other's right to life that she opens a breach in the real in which the human can again make itself felt. This, ultimately, is what rescues her from immersion in matter and in the inhuman.

Le Fils or the monster in his labyrinth

Le Fils provides another variation on the refusal to kill the other. Its hero, a carpenter, works in a centre where released offenders are trained in manual skills. His life has effectively stopped from the moment when, attempting to steal his car radio, a youth had strangled his son who had been on the back seat. Unlike his ex-wife who is to remarry and is expecting another child, he is unable to begin his life again. The Spartan bareness of his workshop and of his flat, their common colour scheme, suggests that, although he may change locations, he is not going anywhere. This is the underlying dynamic of the film. The corridors, stairs, corners and walls that he constantly encounters suggest a character trapped in a labyrinth (Dardenne and Dardenne 2005: 124). An unlikely way out presents itself when Francis, the young murderer, comes to the centre and wants to join his class and become his pupil. The carpenter's powerful body is now traversed by the tension between vengeance and care, between the debt to the past and the duty to the future. He can kill the young man and avenge his murdered child. Or, recognising his right to live, and his need for help, he can become his tutor and guide, thus retying a broken link between generations. His movements and actions oscillate between stalking Francis and training him. Matters come to a head when, having driven him out to a forest to see his brother's timber yard, the hero finally admits that he is the father of the murdered child. Francis flees but is caught and pinned to the ground. It seems as if the hero will strangle him. But, looking into his face, the hero draws back from murder. Putting the rope and tarpaulin that he had perhaps brought to hide a body to positive use, he begins to load timber into his trailer. Silently, Francis begins to help him. Refraining from murder, recognising the right of the other to live, the hero has opened a way out of his labyrinth, a door onto another reality than the one in which he seemed condemned to move.

More than once the Dardenne brothers have said that we live in an age where the fathers devour their sons. Although the constant backdrop to their later work is a sense of the brutality of social interactions in a world governed by competitive individualism, this reference to monstrous fathers suggests that the family plays a central role in their imaginary. The documentaries recorded the dismantling of the old working class and the failing transmission of collective values. Operating in a space where the collective has been demolished, the fictions pursue the study of a crisis of transmission in the narrower sphere of the family. Each of the films figures a failed family cell in which the young can no longer rely on their elders for norms, values, knowledge and protection. *La Promesse* shows an obscene father who, plunged fully into a fallen order, seeks to drag his son into it with him, devouring him, one might say, as a moral being in the process, while encouraging him to devour others in turn. The father in *Rosetta* is absent. The mother, an alcoholic who sells herself to feed her addiction, can only drag her daughter down with her. The upsetting sequence when she leaves her to drown in the pond is a visual expression of a broader inter-generational betrayal, of one generation unwilling or unable to prevent the next from sinking. The sense of an abandoned younger generation proceeds into *Le Fils*, a film which figures two abandoned children, the one left alone on the car seat, the one who murders him. Although the father might seem a simple victim, monstrosity haunts him as, a heavy, menacing figure, he stalks his potential victim. *Le Fils*'s drama of paternity is moved on a generation by *L'Enfant*, a film in which the young father is himself effectively an abandoned child and must reinvent a paternal ethic of responsibility *ex nihilo*.

Representations of the family are typically highly normative with demanding expectations conventionally placed on parents with respect to children. By locating social disintegration and a crisis of transmission within the family, the Dardenne brothers make it all the more shocking, all the more monstrous. They simultaneously give their films a mythical dimension that allows them to reverberate far beyond any purely local frame. Myth and tragedy of course abound with situations in which monstrosity makes itself felt within the family. The story of Kronos who devoured his own children is one that clearly resonates with *La Promesse*, *Le Fils* and *L'Enfant*.[17] But *Le Fils* also has clear echoes of the story of Abraham, the biblical figure who was asked to prove his loyalty to God by sacrificing his own son, and that of Cain and Abel, a foundational story of fratricide (Dardenne 2005: 96). Shakespeare's *Hamlet* also haunts a film where a victim of murder seems to cry out for vengeance (Dardenne 2005: 98–100). The repeated echoes of mythology (or of cultural texts with the status

17 'L'idée que nous avions quand on a fait *La Promesse*, c'était de penser, qu'aujourd'hui, on vivait le temps de Chronos qui mange ses enfants ... qui a peur de perdre la vie en laissant la vie aux autres et qui donc se dépêche de les tuer pour conserver la vie' (Dardenne 2003: 146) ('The idea we had when we made *La Promesse* was that today we were living in the time of Kronos who eats his children ... who is afraid to lose his life by letting others live and so kills them quickly to preserve his own life').

of myth) in the Dardenne brothers' films in general and in *Le Fils* in particular would seem to have a twofold thrust. On the one hand, they underline the sense that we have lurched back into a pre-modern age, an era where norms that seemed to define our civilisation have been lost or remain to be found. On the other hand, abetted by a stylistic asceticism that strips away purely local detail, they help give the films a universal dimension. If a totalising leftist vision is no longer available to translate the social in universalising terms, a mythology made contemporary and given a powerful ethical thrust can perhaps fill the gap.

Ethics in the ruins of politics

In the biblical story of Abraham, God stepped in to prevent the sacrifice by sending a lamb to be slaughtered in place of the child. What, the Dardenne brothers' films ask, can step in to save us from monstrosity now that God has withdrawn from the world? The clear answer is the human. But, in a world where each is the enemy of each and parents devour their children, the human is nowhere to be found. It is something that must be made to reappear through the enforced and traumatic encounter with the other. The centrality of alterity in the Dardenne brothers' work seems tightly linked to their discovery of the writings of the great ethical philosopher, Emmanuel Levinas. For Levinas, the western philosophical tradition, despite its enormous variation, is generally characterised by a refusal of true otherness that is rooted in the centrality of the self, the drive to a totalising knowledge and the imposition of concepts and categories that force the unknown to conform to the shape of the known. The core of the complex and evolving Levinasian project is to place the other rather than the self at the centre and to recognise that, far from being a point of origin, the self is born into a world (of others) that precedes it and in which it must learn to live. It is only by recognising the radical alterity of the other – the other's right to be other and to challenge and escape our categories – that one can move from a state of war, a desire to dominate, towards a state of peace. Levinas's key writings appear in the aftermath of fascism and the Holocaust and are an attempt to provide the foundations of an ethical philosophy that was not knowingly or inadvertently complicit with a totalitarian project of categorisation, domination and extermination.[18] The Dardenne brothers' work belongs to a very different historical period, but what runs through their recent films is a sense that we live in a world where the other's humanity is again denied due to the rise of acquisitive individualism and the murderous competition of all against all. It is for this reason that, taking their cue from Levinas, they place the encounter with the other at the heart of their filmmaking.[19]

Otherness in *La Promesse* has a considerable sociological and philosophical density. Not only do Assita and Amidou come from outside Europe, they retain a connection to extended family ties and to an animist belief system that is in radical contrast to the brute materialism and social isolation of the European characters. In keeping with a general trend towards simplification, the other in *Rosetta* loses this sociological density. Riquet is radically other to Rosetta not because of any ethnic or class difference but simply because he repeatedly tries to help her in a way she cannot understand and which challenges the parameters of a world in which people seem condemned to compete. The young murderer in *Le Fils* is a character similarly without sharp social delineation. He is radically alien to the hero, not because of any identifiable values, but because he has done his family extreme harm, a harm that calls for revenge and thus encapsulates the danger of murder between self and other.

Despite this paring down of otherness, several aspects of the encounter with alterity remain constant from film to film. The first is the other's already mentioned capacity to bring the human back to the surface through an implicit reassertion of the command not to kill. The second is the other's stubborn refusal to disappear and his or her capacity to harass the hero until he or she is recognised. This is expressed perhaps most graphically in *Le Fils* when the murderer slides down a ladder to land on the hero's shoulders, a burden that he

18 Levinas (2003) is the foundation stone of the philosopher's work.

19 A Levinasian ethics clearly underlies the brothers' vision of the contemporary function of (their) art: 'Levinas a écrit dans *Difficile liberté* que l'âme n'est pas possibilité d'immortalité (la mienne) mais l'impossibilité de tuer (autrui). L'art est reconnu par beaucoup comme une manifestation de notre possibilité de d'immortalité ... Pourrait-il être une modalité de l'institution de l'impossibilité de tuer?' (Dardenne 2005: 42) ('Levinas wrote in *Difficult Freedom* that the soul is not the possibility of (my) immortality but the impossibility of killing (the other). Art is recognised by many as a manifestation of our chance to be immortal ... Could it be a way to institute the impossibility of killing?').

cannot bear. Never a mere abstraction, the other is an importuning, disruptive physical presence that must somehow be dealt with. But the other also offers the hero's only hope of salvation, his or her only escape from the inhuman reality that he or she inhabits. It is here also that the echoes of Levinas are strongly felt. If freedom is conventionally seen as something that, emanating from the individual, precedes and must be restrained by the encounter with the other, a deeper freedom in a Levinasian sense flows from being with the other (Caygill 2002: 157–8). All the Dardenne brothers' leading characters are effectively trapped – in inhuman situations, in material flows, in matter, in self-centred survival strategies – until the repeated and enforced encounter with the other enables them to liberate themselves by opening a window onto another more human real.

The Dardenne brothers' cinema is one of action and of the body in its encounter with others and with objects. Its privileging of embodied interaction might suggest that it is a cinema of surfaces and exteriors. Yet its deeper drive is to use visible surfaces not so much to make the invisible appear as to make its invisibility tangible. It is only by so doing that it can make an ethical occult signal its presence. Reminiscent in this of the work of Bresson with its refusal of psychologisation and its relentless focus on external gestures, the brothers' cinema is one that asks that we work from what we are shown to what we cannot see.[20] If each film is driven by an unseen ethical tension, our access to that tension can only come from how it plays out across the bodies of the characters. Thus, for example, in *La Promesse*, Igor seems about to vomit when, reading the signs, the African marabou suggests an ability to name the location of the bodies of the dead. The African characters still have access to an ethico-spiritual transcendence that can find a hidden sense in the material world. The Europeans, on the other hand, bury their guilt just as they bury the body of the man they have caused to die. It is only through Igor's involuntary gesture that the hidden ethical conflict can be forced to the surface. A striking scene in *Le Fils* provides another telling example. It comes when the young killer asks the victim's father, his joinery tutor, to estimate the distance between them and is astonished by the accuracy of the answer. Under-

20 Bresson's hostility to conventional cinematic acting runs through his *Notes on the Cinematographer* (Bresson 1997). For a concise account of the Bressonian 'model' see Reader (2000: 2–4) and for acknowledgement of the clear debt to Bresson see Dardenne (2005: 106).

lining the gulf between the measurable physical distance and the immeasurable moral distance that separates the characters, the film makes the un-representability of the invisible tangible. Moreover, the relationship between the two characters, between tutor and apprentice, straddles an essential tension between two modes of being. If, on the one hand, the tutor's role is to teach his pupil to measure and to name the things around him and thus to situate himself in the physical world, on the other, his task is to take moral responsibility for him. Along similar lines but at a more general level, the Dardenne brothers' heroes exist in the uneasy space between the ontological and the ethical. As ontological action heroes they seek to control their surroundings and risk turning others into mere obstacles. But, as reluctant ethical beings, they are repeatedly made to recognise their responsibility for the other.

Rigorously consistent with itself, the brothers' cinema demands a type of spectatorship that one might also label ethical. The basis of this lies in a detached proximity to the main protagonists. While we are not allowed to hold them at an objectifying distance – to know them, to pin them down – we are also prevented from fully identifying with them. In the same way that the protagonists are forced to recognise their being-with-others, we are forced to be with the characters. This being-with is generated by formal and stylistic choices at the level of character, performance style, action and narrative.[21] Firstly, as the characters exist in the tension between the human and the monstrous, we are simultaneously attracted and repulsed by them. Secondly, because the performances are essentially Bressonian and operate at the level of the bodily surface rather than seeking to project an interiority, the characters resist us and challenge us to decipher them rather than drawing us in. This resistance is accentuated in *Rosetta* and especially *Le Fils* where they are often seen from behind, forcing us to engage with the opacity of bodily exteriority rather than the apparent transparency that a more conventional facial close-up would offer. Thirdly, at the narrative level, the films deliberately leave us one step behind the characters, trying to make sense of actions that, often literally, run ahead of us. Although the typically extended takes might seem to leave us ample time to follow things, the brusque cutting, close framing and extreme camera mobility mean that we are

21 I am indebted to Frampton (2006: 145–7) for the notion of spectatorship in the Dardenne brothers as a being-with.

kept off balance and denied any sense of narrative mastery. Because the camera obsessively tracks the central characters – especially from *Rosetta* onwards – we are moved through story space with them, driven by their actions and reactions in a way that might again suggest fusional accompaniment. Yet, at the same time, we are consistently denied exact point-of-view shots that might invite identification with their (out)look.[22] When they look at or respond to something, we are typically offered a badly aligned shot, one that, often obscured by obstacles, allows us to see only part of what they see and reminds us of the cinematic frame's capacity to mask as well as to reveal.[23] Moved with but one step behind, near but outside, attracted but repulsed, not quite seeing with, we can neither hold the characters at a safe distance nor become them. We are effectively alongside them, yet still forced to be ourselves, as they deal with the ethical tensions with which the films confront them.

An ethics without a politics?

The Dardenne brothers' cinema is one that has remained admirably contemporary of its time and resolutely faithful to those at the bottom of the social pile. Having simultaneously sought to question and preserve the memory of a leftist tradition of opposition at the moment when the transmission of that tradition was in crisis, it then strove, through the development of an ethical cinema, to restore eloquence and sense to a social struggle and suffering deprived of a collective voice. Yet is this account of an ethics that replaces a politics too schematic? Does it obscure a crucial passage through an ethico-political stage where the old politics still made itself felt even as the

22 In a stimulating piece, Houba (2003) shows how the Dardenne brothers' tracking of their characters' movements and gestures is a way to restore a 'voice' to those who are denied access to the language of the dominant.

23 Benoît Dervaux, the brother's habitual cameraman since *La Promesse*, comments: 'Il y a une réflexion avant chaque prise afin d'être volontairement "mal mis" par rapport au personnage de façon à ce que la caméra ne soit pas là où on l'attend ... C'est pour cela qu'on se cogne aux murs, que l'on se prend les portes' (Dervaux 1999: 17) ('Before each take we think about how we can be deliberately awkwardly placed with respect to the character so that the camera is not where one expects it to be ... That's why we knock into walls and are blocked by doors').

new ethics arose? An examination of the underlying dramaturgy of the later films might suggest this was so. *Je pense à vous* showed the transition from an epic collective politics where a 'we' struggled with a 'they' to an emergent ethics where an individual came to the aid of a suffering other. Yet, taking place in opposition to an oppressive third party (the gang-master) and generating an at least temporary solidarity between two workers, this ethical intervention still potentially opens onto a radical politics. Something similar could be said about *La Promesse* and *Rosetta*, both films in which commitment to the other takes place in the presence of an exploitative third party, even if, by the time of the latter film, it no longer seems possible to confront this third person directly and solidarity becomes purely 'solidarity with' rather than 'solidarity against'. With *Le Fils* and its even narrower central cast the oppressive third party disappears. The murder that precedes the film is rooted in a preference for the thing (the car radio) over the other (the boy on the back seat), which again goes to the heart of the contemporary order but no longer seems to open onto an antagonistic construction of the social. The brothers' recent films have been consistent in their commitment to the margins and in their use of them to mount a critique of the centre and the systemic. Yet this consistency should not blind us to a shift from an ethico-political cinema to a more purely ethical one.

If one views the Dardenne brothers within a conventional auteurist framework, there is a temptation to see their work in maturational terms, with the uncertainties of *Je pense à vous* giving way to the mastery of *Rosetta*, *Le Fils* or *L'Enfant*, as suitable stylistic and formal means were honed to give adequate expression to recurrent personal themes. Yet, such a vision is inadequate in two essential ways: firstly, far from exploring the purely personal, the brothers' films have always turned resolutely outwards onto the world; secondly, eminently successful formal vehicles for their own thematic concerns, the early documentaries disrupt any neat sense of linear maturation. An adequate approach to the brothers' cinema cannot account for either its recent evolution or its sharper longer-term discontinuities without reference to the social, political and cinematic contexts within which the brothers operate. Similarly, any evaluation of their work that would seek to be true to its spirit needs not simply to question the adequacy of formal choices to thematic concerns, but must at the same time gauge the ability of those choices and concerns to go to the heart of the contemporary order. Undoubted *auteurs*, the brothers' cinema paradoxically underscores the limitations of a narrowly auteurist approach to film.

References

Austin, Guy (2004), 'The amateur actors of Cannes 1999: a shock to the (star) system', *French Cultural Studies*, 15:3, 251–63.

Bresson, Robert (1997), *Notes on the Cinematographer* (translated by Jonathan Griffin), Copenhagen, Green Integer.

Burdeau, Emmanuel (1999), 'La défricheuse; à propos de *Rosetta* de Luc et Jean-Pierre Dardenne', *Cahiers du cinéma*, 539, 45–6.

Caygill, Howard (2002), *Levinas and the Political*, London, Routledge.

Dardenne, Luc (2003), 'Dans le dos de l'ange de l'histoire' (interview by Pascal Houba), *Multitudes*, 11, 145–57.

Dardenne, Luc (2005), *Au dos de nos images (1991–2005)*, Paris, Éditions du Seuil.

Dardenne, Luc and Dardenne, Jean-Pierre (1999), 'Il faut être dans le cul des choses' (interview by Bernard Benoliel and Serge Toubiana), *Cahiers du cinéma*, 539, 47–53.

Dervaux, Benoît (1999), 'Le regard privilégié' (interview by Philippe Elhem), *L'Image Le Monde*, 1, 16–18.

Frampton, Daniel (2006), *Filmosophy*, London, Wallfower.

Houba, Pascal (2003), 'La parole errante des corps; pratiques de cinéma mineur', *Multitudes*, 11, 135–43.

Levinas, Emmanuel (2003), *Totality and Infinity: An Essay on Exteriority* (translated by Alphonso Lingis), Pittsburgh, Duquesne University Press.

Mélon, Marc-E. and d'Autreppe, Emmanuel (eds) (1996–97), 'Luc et Jean-Pierre Dardenne, vingt ans de travail en cinéma et vidéo', *Revue Belge du cinéma*, 41.

Reader, Keith (2000), *Robert Bresson*, Manchester, Manchester University Press.

4

Close encounters with distant suffering: Michael Haneke's disarming visions

Libby Saxton

No 'we' should be taken for granted when the subject is looking at other people's pain. (Sontag 2003: 7)

In a recent article for the American journal *Film Comment*, Richard Combs argues that Michael Haneke is currently the paradigmatic filmmaker of 'a new European art cinema', whose elusive and shifting terrain defines itself principally 'in terms of what it is not, in opposition to all the image industries' (2002: 28). Haneke's films can be read as a series of polemical correctives to the morally questionable viewing practices and seductive but duplicitous identifications fostered by the mass media in general and mainstream cinema and television in particular. While he is an Austrian director, the deleterious consumer habits and social malaises diagnosed by his films have never been unique to his native country.[1] Moreover, his four most recent films, *Code inconnu: récit incomplet de divers voyages* (*Code Unknown: Incomplete Tales of Several Journeys*, 2000), *La Pianiste* (*The Piano Teacher*, 2001), *Le Temps du loup* (*Time of the Wolf*, 2003) and *Caché* (*Hidden*, 2005), made predominantly in the French language to accommo-

---

1 Although Haneke has described his first three cinematic releases as 'reports on the progressive emotional glaciation of my country', he has also subsequently expressed misgivings about international commentators' haste to dismiss the conditions depicted in these films as specific only to Austria, a move which, in his view, conveniently obscures their wider significance (1992; 2000b: 169–70). Insightful in this context is Combs's rereading of the so-called 'Vergletscherungs-Trilogie' ('glaciation trilogy') as a key stage in the director's continuing journey 'towards a definition of himself as a European filmmaker' (2002: 28).

date French co-producers and a largely French cast, explore a range of quintessentially European anxieties. Haneke is not only following in the footsteps of directors such as Pedro Almodóvar, Theo Angelopoulos, Abbas Kiarostami and Krzysztof Kieślowski in profiting from the privileged funding opportunities and *cinéphile* culture of support for *auteur* filmmakers in France. The French industry and culture of production, particularly in its ambivalence towards American cinema, is also crucial to Haneke's ongoing search for an oppositional space in which to establish himself as a critical commentator on contemporary Europe. At a time when the contingencies of migration and globalisation are troubling what Zygmunt Bauman has called the '*ménage à trois* ... of territory, state and nation' (2003: 132), Haneke's cinema consistently reframes nationally-specific concerns within a transnational enquiry. Aptly, home space and border territory, insides and outsides and concepts of belonging and displacement emerge as recurrent preoccupations in films which are peopled by 'permanently transient' subjects (Bauman 2003: 147) – by migrants, immigrants, refugees, tourists, drifters and passers-by.

While Haneke's unremittingly provocative interventions have invariably divided audiences and fuelled critical debate, particularly in France, a book-length overview of his films has yet to appear in French or English. Commentators have also been slow to take stock of the ways in which his growing body of French-language work is cumulatively redefining his wider cinematic project, quite possibly due to the challenge these films pose to assumptions about authorial coherence, the recurrence of a set palette of authorial motifs notwithstanding. Although these motifs and a highly distinctive style have won Haneke swift recognition as an *auteur* (indeed, his habit of calling his mothers or female leads Anna or Anne, his fathers or male leads Georg or Georges, and their sons and daughters Benny or Ben and Eva respectively suggests a knowingness with regard to auteurist critical agendas), his subversive forays into a diverse range of genres (including the thriller, melodrama, literary adaptation and disaster movie) test the limits of traditional concepts of authorial continuity. Furthermore, the transnational dimension of his work calls into question the historically close relationship between discourses of authorship and national identity. A reassessment of Haneke's cinema and auteurist credentials is timely in the light of the new trends and shifts in focus emerging in the French-language films. While they revisit territory currently interesting French filmmakers, it is not my intention here to attempt to contextualise them within the thematic and stylistic tendencies of contemporary French cinema (an interpretive *telos* actively resisted by the director, who finds himself no more 'at home' within French than within Austrian cinema). Haneke, who studied philosophy, psychology and theatre and subsequently worked as a theatre and television director, draws on a broad European cultural heritage, including the films of Robert Bresson and Michelangelo Antonioni, the literature of Franz Kafka and Thomas Bernhard and the music of an eclectic range of composers, a heritage that informs his commentary on the postcolonial European landscape.

Critical debate around Haneke's work and authorial status has focused, on the one hand, on the allegedly unrelieved pessimism, even 'nihilism', of his vision of contemporary social relations as sundered, atomised and alienated, and, on the other, on his purportedly sadistic predilection for implicating his viewers in unpalatable depictions of mindless violence. Haneke has alternately been acclaimed as an uncompromising moralist and taken to task for excessive and punitive didacticism. A more compelling and productive line of enquiry at the present juncture, I would suggest, pertains to the fragile, transitory, liquid ethical bonds which survive in a diegetic reality where intersubjective relations are increasingly mediated by technology. While Haneke's films remain dubious about the continued viability of traditional conceptions of community and solidarity in an era of multiculturalism and globalised mass media, their traumatised, vulnerable protagonists are often driven by a desire to forge new connections and a search for new forms of intimacy. This search has little to do with the positivistic ethical project decried by those who condemn Haneke's reactionary moralising. Rather, his cinema tentatively embraces what Paul Arthur has described as 'a reluctant ethics framed largely through negation' (2005: 28).

This chapter explores the ways in which *Code inconnu*, *La Pianiste*, *Le Temps du loup* and *Caché* reconceptualise ethical relations and responsibilities in an image-saturated culture bereft of moral certainties and stable cause and effect relationships. I am interested here, more precisely, in two forms of relations, at once distinct and interdependent: firstly, those between Haneke's on-screen protagonists and, secondly, those between viewers and his images. In recurrently casting their protagonists as spectators, as subjects defined by visually mediated encounters, his films reconfigure self–other relations in terms of ways of looking and viewing practices. As they are incorporated into his cinema, the competing technologies of television, videotape and CCTV – ironically, technologies that were designed to facilitate communication – are implicated in a progressive deterioration of the quality, transparency and humanity of intersubjective exchanges. Haneke is particularly suspicious of the blinkered gaze licensed by the mainstream media, which, in his account, tend to 'falsify' and 'manipulate' reality by allowing only 'les images les plus spectaculaires, les plus choquantes'[2] to pass into circulation. The distorted perspectives which result exacerbate the moral disorientation engendered, above all, by the perpetual televisual looping of images of distant suffering. Selected and packaged for convenient and compliant consumption, these images tend to install in the western viewer little more than a pervasive sense of guilt and a permanent 'mauvaise conscience' (see, for example, Haneke 2005a).

Haneke's aversion to such processes of mediation and concomitant faith in cinema as a site of resistance to their pernicious influence intersect with the concerns of debates in recent scholarship in a number of illuminating ways. In *La Souffrance à distance*, the sociologist Luc Boltanski has analysed the uneasy moral position of a 'spectateur éloigné et abrité'[3] contemplating mediated spectacles of suffering from afar (1993: 42). Drawing on Hannah Arendt's account of an evolving 'politics of pity', Boltanski seeks to identify the moral demands that are placed on this spectator by examining the relationship between contemplation and action, asking how diffident observers might transform themselves into committed actors. The cultural critic Geoffrey Hartman has pursued related questions in an important recent article on the transmission of testimony and trauma in contemporary visual culture. According to Hartman, we are positioned by the media as 'impotent involuntary spectators' of suffering of which 'it is no longer possible not to know'. One of the consequences of this traumatic knowledge – what Hartman, whose account coincides with Haneke's at this juncture, calls 'tele-suffering' – is a 'secondary traumatisation, ... a guilt, perhaps shame, which the knowledge of evil, or simply of such suffering, implants' (2000: 12).

While Boltanski is concerned principally with the mass media,

2 'the most spectacular, shocking images'.
3 'distant and sheltered spectator'.

and Hartman with the ways in which videographic testimony can counteract their deleterious 'unreality-effect' (2000: 4), the film critic Serge Daney explores the possibility that cinema can expose the moral dilemmas facing contemporary spectators by revealing relationships and obligations which other media habitually work to conceal or elide. In *Devant la recrudescence des vols de sacs à main*, Daney posits an opposition between his *bête noire*, the inexhaustible flood of television images that he calls 'le visuel', and 'l'image', which is unique to cinema. The former is defined by the unitary perspective inscribed in its images: '[le] *point de vue du pouvoir*, c'est-à-dire d'un champ sans contrechamp (d'un champ qui annihile son contrechamp)'; '[au] visuel ... il ne ... manque rien, il est clos, en boucle, ... à l'image du spectacle pornographique' (1991: 185, 192).[4] Daney suggests, however, that the homogenising closure and symbolic violence of 'le visuel' can be redressed by 'l'image', which is defined, in contrast, by heterogeneity and lack, and thus 'vouée à témoigner d'une certaine *altérité*' (1991: 193).[5]

Boltanski's analysis of the moral dimensions of spectatorship, Hartman's reflections on spectatorial guilt and trauma and Daney's discussion of the redemptive potential of the cinematic image shed light on some of the challenging and prescient insights of Haneke's work. The free circulation of the alien image-systems of 'le visuel' within his cinematic images reveals the alterity and difference routinely suppressed by the former and the contrasting viewing positions made available by each. 'Distant spectators' of the kind that preoccupy Boltanski and Hartman at once populate and are interpellated by Haneke's films, which, with the notable exception of *Le Temps du loup*, are punctuated by contemporary television or radio reports about catastrophes taking place elsewhere. Symptomatically, however, these reports often fail to sustain the attention of the on-screen viewers, calling into question the temporalities of the 'secondary traumatisation' described by Hartman. Mediated suffering is consumed distractedly by the protagonists of the 'Vergletscherungs-Trilogie' ('glaciation trilogy') which brought Haneke to international prominence (comprising *Der siebente Kontinent* (*The Seventh Continent*, 1989), *Benny's Video* (1992) and *71 Fragmente einer Chronologie*

---

4 '[the] *point of view of power*, in other words, of a shot without a counter-shot (of a shot which annihilates its counter-shot)'; '*le visuel* ... lacks nothing, it is a closed system, a feedback loop ... in the image of a pornographic spectacle'.

5 'dedicated to bearing witness to a certain *alterity*'.

des Zufalls (*71 Fragments of a Chronology of Chance*, 1994)). Haneke's inventive contribution to the portmanteau film *Lumière et compagnie* (*Lumière and Company*, 1995) raises further questions about the nature of spectatorial attention and distraction. Shot with the Lumière brothers' original 1895 *Cinématographe*, Haneke's fifty-two-second montage consists solely of recycled televisual fragments, which mock, in their eclecticism, what Hartman names our 'iconomania' and the indiscriminate channel-grazing which is its unfortunate corollary (2000: 1).

The multiple frames, screens and lenses which vie for attention in Haneke's cinema mediate access to the realities of pain and trauma, even to the reality of the other's body. The viewing habits of his protagonists are shown to derealise and anaesthetise, alienate and dehumanise, commodify and objectify. In reframing the small screen on the big screen, however, his films enjoin their audience to accept the moral responsibilities identified by Boltanski but routinely shirked by the on-screen spectators. Indeed, I want to argue here that Haneke's films work to cultivate more intimate encounters with distant suffering and violence by reinvesting them cinematically with those real, physical properties of which they are drained the moment they enter the media flux: 'I try to give back to violence that which it truly is: pain, injury to another' (Haneke, cited in Frey 2003). This concern to reveal the material reality of bodily violation also implicates the body of the viewer-witness, a body habitually preserved as inviolable by the signifying procedures of dominant forms of cinema. In according a spectrum of spectators physical presence on-screen, Haneke's films insist on spectatorship as an embodied, corporealised experience, as an encounter between vulnerable bodies.

Moreover, as an antidote to the progressive 'incapacitation of the spectator' effected by the mainstream media, Haneke asserts that he seeks to nurture an 'interactive' viewer engaged in a critical dialogue with his sounds and images: 'A film's essential feature, its criterion of quality, should be its ability to become the productive centre of an interactive process' (Haneke 1992; 2000a: 171). In theory, that is, according to the director's expansive statements of authorial intent, the ethical value of such 'interactivity' would reside in its potential at once to re-empower and disarm the spectator. Not only would it require concentration and interpretive effort in place of the passive consumption promoted by films which merely perpetuate an 'aesthetics of distraction', it would also induce a 'productive unease' in place of the reassuring certainties propagated by the escapist mainstream (Haneke 2000b: 160; 1996: 10).

In practice, however, as several critics have noticed, Haneke's theoretical prioritisation of spectatorial work and agency is potentially undermined by his films' tendency to manipulate or wilfully mislead their viewers. Placing his French-language films in dialogue with the different accounts of spectatorship outlined above, including the director's own, the readings that follow explore the ways in which these films intervene in current debates about the ethical dimensions of viewing, challenging our preconceptions about viewing practices, relations and positions. Spectatorship is reconfigured in Haneke's work as a series of hazardous and disconcerting but always potentially ethical encounters, events or crises.

Myopic visions: *Code inconnu: récit incomplet de divers voyages*

In the context of a body of work which censures the media's liability to keep others' suffering at a comfortable distance, Haneke's first French-language film, *Code inconnu*, might be read as an attempt to intervene in and reverse this process. As the director turns his attention to the social implications of contemporary migratory flows, scenes of dispossession formerly confined to the small screen in his films find their way onto the big screen. Following in the footsteps of Marian who flees from Romania to Austria in *71 Fragmente*, refugees, asylum-seekers, legal and illegal immigrants and economic migrants are beginning to invade Haneke's diegetic fictions. Moreover, as Jörg Metelmann points out, *Code inconnu* is the first of the director's films on which the realities of war impinge directly, via the character of Georges, a war photographer, rather than entering the fiction indirectly through the media (2003: 266).

Georges's traumatic viewing position as an eyewitness to atrocity confronts him with moral dilemmas about professional distance and personal involvement and the problem of western compassion fatigue. Early on in the film, the flow of moving images is interrupted by a montage of still shots depicting ruined buildings, anguished faces, wounded and dying bodies and corpses in various states of decomposition, which we recognise as photographs taken by Georges in Kosovo. These images are accompanied on the soundtrack by a fragment from one of his letters to Anne, in which he admits aborting earlier attempts to write to her from the war zone: 'Je ne savais pas quoi dire'.[6] The disjunctive relationship between word and image in this sequence is disconcerting for viewers accustomed to the horrors of distant suffering being explained, contained and made more digestible by a televisual voice-over. Brigitte Peucker has argued that the emotionless voices of television commentators 'render a sanitised version of the real precisely where the spectator has come to believe s/he has access to its immediacy'. In this respect, television coverage 'works hard to keep the shock of catastrophe at bay' (2000: 179). Combs, pursuing an intersecting line of enquiry, notes that the war in former Yugoslavia is 'a constant reference point for Haneke, as an example of irreducible, uncontainable, "real" violence, the real we can't grasp through TV' (2002: 26). Haneke's cinematic reframing of Georges's photographs seeks to make this violence more real, more tangible and more unpalatable. The eruption of real suffering and real death temporarily suspends the diegetic fictions, repositioning the spectator as a witness to – rather than consumer of – history, in line with the ethical priorities posited by Boltanski, Hartman and Daney.

In counterpoint to these mediated confrontations, the 'divers voyages' depicted in *Code inconnu* are connected by face-to-face encounters of the unpredictable kind fostered by urban topography. Hard to avoid in a Paris where everybody is in transit, where even those reduced to begging on the streets are constantly being moved on, these chance meetings bring the film's protagonists into visual contact and close physical proximity with others' distress. Just as these encounters confront the protagonists with a series of moral choices, so they confront the viewers with ethical questions about responsibility, hospitality, involvement and indifference – or what Stéphane Goudet terms 'le repli et l'ouverture à l'autre' (2000: 23).[7]

The film's prologue and epilogue pose these questions in relation to spectatorship by setting up models of fractured viewing relations where the desire to know and understand the other remains frustrated. 'Seul?' 'Cachette?' 'La mauvaise conscience?' 'Triste?' 'Emprisonné?':[8] the sign-language interpretations hazarded by the on-screen audience

6 'I didn't know what to say'.
7 'withdrawal from and openness to the other'.
8 'Alone?' 'Hiding place?' 'Guilty?' 'Sad?' 'Imprisoned?'

of hearing-impaired children as they ponder the meaning of their friend's enigmatic charade anticipate our own speculations about the themes which bind together the film's disparate narratives. Yet each interpretation is swiftly refuted by the miming girl, whose anguished gestures, like those of the boy in the concluding sequence, remain undeciphered and undecidable. This indefinite deferral of meaning appears to frame the action as a commentary on the potentially unbridgeable intersubjective distances that threaten our bids to communicate with others, visually or otherwise. At the same time, of course, it also challenges the legitimacy of our desire to impose any such overarching interpretation on the film.

The illegible bodies of these children announce Haneke's interest in occasions when the bodily senses integral to interpersonal exchanges are dulled, impaired or break down. The faulty models of communication offered by the film explore metaphors not only of hearing, deafness and touch but also of vision and blindness. Whereas in *Der siebente Kontinent*, Eva, misled by a newspaper headline, feigns blindness in the false hope that it will dispel her sense of isolation, in *Code inconnu*, attempts to establish connections with others are threatened by a succession of failures to see, both literal and metaphorical. Indeed, while the film's investigations of photography, filmmaking and acting foreground regimes of looking and being looked at, contemporary European urban multiculturalism is staged here as a drama predominantly of looking *away* and being *over*looked. This drama is played out at two sites in the film: on-screen and off-screen. Wrapped up in their own concerns, the on-screen protagonists are all too often liable to turn a blind eye to the spectacle of others' disempowerment, or quite simply too short-sighted to notice it. The film's multiple narratives thus intersect, on the screen, in a series of missed encounters foreclosed by failures of perception and forms of blindness. At the same time, however, as we shall see, the film's form also calls into question the spaces between and outside the frames, and, with them, the habitually privileged gaze of the film spectator.

Foreclosed encounters with strangers and the guilt and shame they can induce in both parties are the subject of two stories told towards the end of the film by Maria, a middle-aged Romanian woman who spends periods *sans papiers* on the streets of Paris gathering funds to send back to her family. In the first story, which takes place in Certeze, she remembers giving money to a Roma beggar-woman whose dirtiness so disgusted her that she ran home to wash her hands. The second story replays the first with the roles reversed. A well-dressed man approaches Maria on the Boulevard St Germain, visibly blanches and recoils as he catches sight of the filth on her outstretched hand, and drops his twenty-franc note hurriedly in her lap in order to avoid touching her. At once utterly banal, if mildly embarrassing (for the benefactor) and absolutely traumatic (for the recipient), as Maria reveals, these structurally identical encounters attest to the conflicting but often coexisting impulses provoked by the sight of others in need or pain. The passer-by's divergent reactions to Maria's plight and dirty hands – just like her own ambivalent response to the Roma woman – suggest a humanitarian desire to assist betrayed by an involuntarily dehumanising suspicion of bodies that bear marks of difference or disempowerment, marks which are liable to blind the beholder to signs of shared humanity and vulnerability.

Code inconnu can be read as a series of variations on this theme. The conflicted actions of Maria and her benefactor are symptomatic of one of the central targets of the film's political and ethical critique: a self-serving if involuntary blindness or blinkeredness with regard to the fate of those on the margins which – albeit inadvertently – colludes in the mechanisms of marginalisation. Even the ostensibly liberal and tolerant couple Anne and Georges remain oblivious, whether by oversight or intention, to much of the suffering around them. What is more, on the occasions when this suffering *is* perceived, attempts to assume responsibility and intervene or assist, such as Anne's half-hearted investigation of the child abuse she suspects is taking place in a neighbouring apartment, prove largely ineffectual. Or, worse, like Amadou's noble but misjudged endeavour to protect Maria's dignity when she is insulted by Jean, they have unforeseen adverse consequences. In its multiple ramifications, this is one of a number of confrontations in the film that recall Slavoj Žižek's provocative condemnation of liberal multiculturalism, which, in his account, tolerates the other only so long as it remains 'aseptic', 'fascinating', exotic (and, we might add, remains safely within the confines of the televisual frame). As soon as the other becomes 'real', the multicultural gaze adopts a 'patronising Eurocentrist distance' inflected by a disavowed racism (1999: 219, 216). Endemic to all levels of the multicultural society portrayed by *Code inconnu*, it would seem, is a myopic, inhospitable vision that works to keep the other's suffering at bay.

If Georges encounters difficulties in speaking about his work, two sequences in the second half of the film offer a haunting retrospective commentary on the Kosovo images, as well as an insight into the distances which foreclose the face-to-face encounters staged by the fiction. In the first sequence, Georges is shown surreptitiously taking snapshots of unsuspecting fellow travellers on the metro in Paris. The second, which can be read as the counter-shot of the first, consists of a montage of black-and-white photographic portraits of men and women of various ages and ethnicities, over which Georges reads from a letter describing his experiences in Afghanistan where he was held captive by Taliban fighters. The photographs are borrowed from a book by the war photographer Luc Delahaye entitled *L'Autre* (1999), a collection of ninety portraits of metro passengers taken using a hidden camera and published without the authorisation of the subjects, accompanied by a text by Jean Baudrillard. *L'Autre* has featured in current debates about *le droit à l'image* in France. In capturing the other unawares, in an instant of utter vulnerability, Georges's/Delahaye's subterfuge arouses familiar moral qualms about voyeurism, the rights of photographic subjects and the hierarchical relationships between subject and object of the look. While the images of devastation in the Balkans (also the work of Delahaye) serve a documentary and testimonial function, Francine's doubts about their necessity and efficacy notwithstanding, the portraits stolen on the metro seem to belong to a covert regime of surveillance, anticipating the work of the hidden filmmaker in *Caché*. Viewed in parallel, however, the two photographic montages offer an eloquent testimony to the uneasy dialectics of distance and involvement that so often inflect visual encounters with alterity.

Something is withheld from our gaze in the portraiture, just as it is in Haneke's fictional fragments, and in the face-to-face encounters they narrate. Indeed, *Code inconnu* constantly refocuses our attention on that which eludes our look – on the sites of non-seeing which structure spectatorship. Moreover, in counterpoint to the myopic vision of many of its protagonists, the film suggests that certain forms of blindness are a precondition for the cinematic revelation of truth. These are the grounds on which Haneke dismisses the complete disclosure of reality falsely promised by escapist cinema (epitomised here by the *film policier* in which Anne is starring): 'Le cinéma de distraction prétend que nous pouvons montrer la réalité dans sa totalité, ce qui est faux. Si le cinéma veut être responsable, c'est-à-dire être un art véritable, il est obligé de se rendre compte que notre perception du monde est naturellement fragmentée' (2000c: 25).[9] Cinema, in this account, has a responsibility to reveal our inability to perceive reality in its totality, all at once, as a continuous whole. From this perspective, the conspicuous formal fragmentation of *Code inconnu* (like the fractured narratives of many of Haneke's films, most notably *Der siebente Kontinent*, *71 Fragmente* and *Das Schloß* (*The Castle*, 1997)) can be read as an ethical strategy. As its subtitle acknowledges, the film's narrative fragments refuse to add up to a coherent, seamless whole. Their bewildering plurality and incompletion are accentuated by the silent two-second black leaders which separate them. The temporarily empty, dark screen implies an ethical gesture of refusal, a withdrawal from the ubiquitous 'visuel' and its regime of permanent visibility. Like the televisual snow which terminates the flow of images in *Der siebente Kontinent*, the repeated interruption of the image-chain in *Code inconnu* disrupts those processes of bodily sense-making on which cinema habitually relies; just as the absence of sound confounds our sense of hearing, so the absence of light obfuscates our sense of sight.

How, then, are we to 'interact' with these non-images? Haneke claims they buy us thinking time (2000c: 27). An absence that waits to be filled with light and presence, the blank screen also persists as a space of projection, allowing the free-play of the intellect and the imagination. In making the cut visible and foregrounding the film's materiality and constructedness, the black leaders invite us to attend to the margins of blindness which frame our 'regard fragmenté'[10] in the cinema – and in the world beyond (2000c: 25). In revealing these blindspots Haneke sharpens our vision. *Code inconnu* offers its viewers some of the intimate insights into alterity that elude its protagonists precisely by acknowledging the impossibility of perceiving the irreducible reality of the other in its totality.

9 'Escapist cinema claims that we can show reality in its totality, which isn't true. If cinema is to be responsible, that's to say, if it's to be true art, it's obliged to realise that our perception of the world is naturally fragmented'.
10 'fragmented gaze'.

Apocalypse now: *La Pianiste* and *Le Temps du loup*

Haneke's next two films revisit territory familiar from the 'Vergletscherungs-Trilogie' and *Funny Games* (1997), depicting characters isolated and viewing relations traumatised by unpredictable outbursts of radical violence. Despite this continuity, both films have been discussed as anomalies in Haneke's filmography to date. *La Pianiste*, a loose adaptation of Elfriede Jelinek's novel *Die Klavierspielerin* (1983), is Haneke's first sustained investigation of gender, sexuality and sensuous desire. *Le Temps du loup* appears to mark another departure, leaping forward into a post-apocalyptic future where the circulation of images and capital has ceded to the circulation of bodies locked in a primitive fight for survival. But the two films' contrasting physical terrains – late twentieth-century Vienna and a multi-lingual rural wilderness somewhere in Europe – conceal common psychological and social territory. If what Christopher Sharrett describes as the 'devastated emotional landscape' of *La Pianiste* assumes a material form in the wasteland traversed by the protagonists of *Le Temps du loup*, Anna, Eva and Ben are also, like Erika, at risk of becoming trapped by suffering in an emotional desert (2002: 39). Furthermore, the protagonists of both films attempt to escape isolation by finding new ways of reaching out to others in worlds where conventional bourgeois moral values are becoming increasingly obsolescent.

Both films situate the collapse of traditional morality within the context of the precarious legacy of western civilisation, its institutions and culture. If *La Pianiste* reveals this culture to be straining at the seams, no longer able to repress its discontents, *Le Temps du loup* imagines the socio-political fallout of its implosion. In both cases, moreover, the immediate locus of this fallout is the anchoring institution of the white, middle-class, nuclear family, identified by Haneke as 'the germinating cell for all conflicts' (2003: 31). In his work over the years, this normative family has often been the stage where apocalyptic scenarios are compulsively rehearsed, whether the agent of violence invades from the outside or is already an insider. What is particularly unnerving about the violence in *Der siebente Kontinent*, *Benny's Video*, *Funny Games*, *Le Temps du loup* and *Caché* is that it erupts where least expected: into the heart of the organic family unit and its home. In these films domestic familial space is no longer a safe space, a sanctuary from a threatening exterior. Instead, it has become, literally, a death-trap, liable to implode at any moment.

The normative family, then, is recurrently fantasised by Haneke only to be dispersed, dismembered or decimated. This serial configuration not only reveals the frail, ephemeral nature of the nuclear construct; it also allows Haneke to scrutinise what withstands the onslaught and to examine how familial bonds bear up to the centrifugal forces to which, today, they are increasingly subjected. The story of the childless Austrian couple who deliberate over whether to adopt an Austrian or Romanian child in *71 Fragmente* signals an interest in the flexible and permeable boundaries of modern familial permutations, which Haneke pursues further in *La Pianiste*, *Le Temps du loup* and, later, *Caché*. Rather than organic nuclear units, Erika and her mother in *La Pianiste* and Anna, Eva and Ben in *Le Temps du loup* form fragmented, decentred families haunted by the absence of the father. In depicting their struggles for survival these films challenge normative conceptions of familial identities, revealing the family as a series of fluid relations and identifications structured and sundered by conflicting desires and fears.

La Pianiste has been read, after Lacan, as a film about 'the impossibility of desire in general and female sexuality in particular' (Champagne 2002). Erika's symbiotic bond with her intractable, pre-Oedipal mother precludes the possibility of emotional intimacy not only between mother and daughter but also with those outside the family dyad, including Erika's lover, Walter. While her confession to him 'je n'ai pas de sentiments'[11] carries echoes of the 'emotional glaciation' that besets the protagonists of Haneke's trilogy, what distinguishes Erika from them is the persistence and irreducibility of her desire to feel. Her habits of self-mutilation and voyeurism attest to a longing for bodily sensation and sensory experience which is only fuelled by her inability to take pleasure in the arms of another. This is a film where the other's touch is merely a prelude to nausea or violence. Consequently, Erika seeks refuge in fantasy, which she, like Benny in the second film of the trilogy, is apt to confuse with reality. What is more, insofar as they involve scenarios of imprisonment and bondage, her fantasies suggest a masochistic compulsion to restage her predicament.

The film visualises Erika's psychological prison in terms of spatial relations. Haneke, departing from Jelinek's text, traps his protagonist

11 'I have no feelings'.

within a hermetically sealed world of sterile interiors where walls and doors have eclipsed sky and horizon. These claustrophobic spaces bear an uncanny resemblance to the terrifying windowless rooms in which Anne finds herself confined in the *film policier* in *Code inconnu*, the bedroom in *Benny's Video* which is sealed off from the outside world by permanently drawn blinds, and the holiday home in *Funny Games* from which Schorschi is prevented from escaping by security gates. Like many of Haneke's protagonists, Erika does not so much inhabit the spaces through which she moves as she finds herself imprisoned by them. Even the cramped domestic space she shares with her mother affords neither sanctuary nor privacy; she is at once 'homeless' and unable to escape from a home that has been rendered uninhabitable.

Spatial relations, however, do not fully determine viewing relations in this film. Stefan Grisseman observes that Erika is often shown in places associated either with looking (the drive-in movie, the pay-per-view video booth) or with being looked at (the concert stage, the rehearsal and performance rooms) (2001: 18). Like Anne in *Code inconnu*, Erika, as a performer, is caught within a system of appraising gazes presided over, here, by the controlling gaze of her mother. But not only does she endeavour to withdraw herself from this regime, for example, by barricading her door against her mother, or simply by turning her back on the camera; she also attempts to reappropriate the gaze as a means of resistance. Erika's viewing habits differ markedly from her mother's. Prior to Walter's visits, the third defining presence in their apartment is the television, whose intrusive images sometimes occupy the whole cinematic screen, and whose sounds – a stand-in, in Sharrett's reading, for the absent patriarchal voice (2002: 39) – supply the soundtrack to the domestic drama. While her mother consumes a diet of soaps and game-shows, Erika is irritated by the incessant noise and images to the point that she requests her mother's permission to switch them off (echoing Anna's reaction to her son's death in *Funny Games*). Whereas the heroine of Jelinek's novel 'longs for her soft TV armchair behind a locked door' (Jelinek 1983: 76), in Haneke's film, Erika seeks out visual pleasures of a different kind.

The multiple pornographic scenarios on the split screen in the video booth she visits position her as a consumer with a choice. At the drive-in movie once again a variety of spectacles vie for her attention; this time it is not the escapist passion on the screen that interests Erika so much as the real bodies copulating in the darkened cars around her. Yet if she takes evident pleasure in reappropriating the voyeuristic, fetishistic 'male gaze' which has long preoccupied feminist film theorists, the extent to which the film affirms this move as a subversive strategy remains questionable. Rather than liberating her from the networks of gazes and spaces that constrict her, Erika's penchant for voyeurism compounds her isolation. What is denied to the voyeur, who desires to look secretly, to see without being seen, is the pleasure of the touch of the other.

At the same time, however, the film's *mise en scène* and camera-work collude, compassionately, in Erika's bids for autonomy. In *Der siebente Kontinent*, the breakdown of intersubjective relations is evoked by disorientating close-ups of hands and objects which banish the protagonists' faces into off-screen space. *La Pianiste*, by contrast, is replete with medium and close-up shots of Erika's face, which insist on her gaze as she observes and listens to others and stares longingly out of windows, positioning her as subject rather than object of the look. Moreover, like Georges's portraits in *Code inconnu*, these shots withhold more than they reveal. The micro-movements that animate Isabelle Huppert's exceptionally expressive face remain curiously illegible. Even her anguished grimace as the cold steel of the kitchen knife enters the soft flesh of her shoulder is replaced in the blink of an eye by her routine impassivity, heightening the ambiguity of the film's conclusion. The plurality and contradictions of critical readings of the rape scene attest, in part at least, to the difficulty of reading a face that barely registers pain or pleasure (see, for example, Champagne 2002; Hutchison 2003; Wood 2002: 61). John Champagne has suggested that the visual focus on Erika's face places us 'in the position of the porn spectator who searches for visible evidence of female pleasure and the reassurance that men can provide such pleasure' (2002).[12] But Haneke, for reasons I discuss below, ensures that such a viewing position is an entirely ungratifying one. Erika's face is less a window on her soul than a mask which conceals it from sight, or a blank screen which, like so many of Haneke's images, solicits the specta-tor's projections.

In their reluctance to lay bare subjectivity, to expose interiority,

12 For an account of hard core pornography as an already failed attempt to make invisible female bodily pleasure visible through its involuntary confession, see Linda Williams (1989: 48–51).

the shots of Erika's face confirm Haneke's reputation as a filmmaker who refuses to indulge his audience's desire for psychological explanations on the grounds that these are always potentially reductive. *Le Temps du loup* is, if anything, even more hesitant and restrained in its revelation of subjectivity. As in *La Pianiste*, the fragile, precarious nature of familial bonds is figured here by a relay of silent, screen-like gazes which manifest intersubjective distance as much as proximity. Furthermore, even as they draw us in, the images of the later film work persistently to disturb our vision, not only frustrating our desire for psychological insights but also intermittently impeding visual contact with the bodies on the screen.

The reticence of its images notwithstanding, *Le Temps du loup* might be read as Haneke's most concerted attempt to date to confront us with the material realities of the distant catastrophes that we in the western world are accustomed to witnessing only on the small screen. The unwelcome sense of *déjà-vu* prompted by the opening sequence, which echoes the beginning of *Funny Games*, is soon revealed as a false lead. As the narrative unfolds, Georges's abrupt, silent, abject death at the hands of the intruders he disturbs in the family's holiday home is recontextualised as an aftershock of a larger-scale catastrophe which took place some time before the opening credits. If the film begins with an end – the death of the father – it also opens, in effect, *after* the end. This end that has already happened emerges as its absent subject, at once narrative origin and blindspot. Just as *La Pianiste* systematically breaks with the generic conventions of the melodrama and *Funny Games* and *Caché* with those of the thriller, so *Le Temps du loup* implicitly parodies the disaster movie by relegating the spectacle of the apocalyptic event to an unlocatable off-screen (or pre-screen) space. Unrepresented and unidentified, it is spoken of only obliquely via allusions to shortages, rationing and contamination. While the aural and visual clues supplied by the film point, perhaps, to the fallout of a Hiroshima or a Chernobyl, and assume particular resonance in the wake of the events of 11 September 2001 and Hurricane Katrina, for example, the film refuses to legitimise any one of these interpretations. Instead, in declining to name the catastrophe, it works to challenge the assumption of western viewers, bolstered by television, that disasters only ever happen 'elsewhere'.

The complacence of such 'distant spectators' is shaken here by the unfamiliar sight of a white, European, middle-class family splintered by violence, divested of all the trappings of the bourgeoisie and forced to live as refugees in their own country. Removed without warning from the regime of consumable objects and images that ensnares the protagonists of Haneke's other films, Anna, Eva and Ben find themselves exposed for the first time to the traumas of real, non-mediated space. In the post-apocalyptic present there is, after all, no longer any electricity to feed the television. The collapse of systems of mediation coincides with the breakdown of law and order. In the 'time of the wolf', the patriarchal constructs and social conventions that might otherwise shield the family from an increasingly foreign and inhospitable environment have ceased to function. Neighbourly bonds are severed, moral codes such as hospitality and altruism no longer apply, and multicultural tolerance has given way to inter-ethnic hostility.

Just as the disintegration of moral paradigms reshapes familial bonds according to new ethical priorities, as witnessed in particular by the enigmatic behaviour of Ben, so viewing relations too are restructured by the aftershocks of the catastrophe. Much of the film is shot at night, with minimal artificial lighting. Consequently, in certain key sequences, all that is visible in the otherwise impenetrable darkness on the screen are the contours of part of a face lit by the flickering flame of a cigarette lighter, candle or flare. In daytime scenes, too, visibility is often impaired by a blanket of mist, or simply by the film's washed-out visual palette. Haneke paints his future-present landscape in shades of grey and beige; at times even the human body begins to take on a monochrome, drained, almost transparent quality which seems to anticipate its impending extinction. This is a film that will not allow us simply to bathe passively in the glow of projected light but requires us instead constantly to *strain to see*. Just as liable to lose our bearings as its protagonists, we share in their bewilderment and disorientation.

What is more, in place of close-ups and subjective camerawork, the image-track is dominated by prolonged unbroken takes from a static camera which compound the viewers' unease. Such shots draw us into the dilated temporality or 'dead time' of endless waiting and permanently frustrated expectation endured by the protagonists themselves as they watch for a train to transport them back to the city. Haneke has regularly exploited the potential of the extended sequence shot to liberate our vision from the constrictive viewing habits fostered by television and mainstream cinema. This is the function, for example, of the seemingly interminable stationary takes of children leaping over gymnastic vaulting-blocks in *Der siebente Kontinent*, of the video monitor during the girl's death agonies in *Benny's Video*, of the table tennis training session and the game of Pick a Stick in *71 Fragmente* and of the blood-spattered television and living room after the first murder in *Funny Games*. In their deference to real time, such shots frame the scene for longer than is strictly necessary for the advancement of the narrative or entirely comfortable for an audience accustomed to rapid televisual montage and channel-hopping. Haneke explains the fruits of such discomfort as follows:

> The faster something is shown, the less able you are to perceive it as an object occupying a space in physical reality ... Television accelerates experience, but one needs time to understand what one sees, which the current media disallows ... Cinema still has the capacity, I think, to let us experience the world anew. The long take is an esthetic means to accomplish this by its particular emphasis ... Of course, film is always manipulation, but if each scene is only one shot, then, I think, there is at least less of a sense of *time* being manipulated when one tries to stay close to a 'real time' framework. The reduction of montage to a minimum also tends to shift responsibility back to the viewer in that more contemplation is required. (2003: 31)

For Haneke, it is only when the viewer is forced to contemplate an object in real time at such length that he or she 'traverse[s] the threshold of boredom' that he or she 'actually begins to watch' (2001a: 182). The director's reflections on this topic recall André Bazin's (pre-televisual) admiration for the long take in its capacity to preserve temporal and spatial unity. Montage is suspect in Bazin's account since cinema should be judged according not to 'ce qu'elle *ajoute* à la réalité mais ... ce qu'elle en *révèle*' (1958: 135).[13] Certainly, in allowing profilmic reality to unfold in real time, Haneke's long takes imply the off-screen presence of a neutral observer and documenter, particularly when the camera remains motionless. Yet this impression often proves misleading; indeed, Bazin's celebration of transparent revelation remains incompatible with Haneke's embrace of cinema as an art, first and foremost, of manipulation (see, for example, Haneke 2000c: 26; 2001a: 186). As he acknowledges above, the attempt to minimise

13 'what it *adds* to reality but ... what it *reveals of* it'.

the manipulation of time merely engenders other forms of artifice and intervention. At the same time, both Haneke's films and Bazin's writings are informed by an interest in the complexities of spectatorial perception and engagement. Haneke's elongated sequence shots challenge the viewer by defamiliarising the passage of time itself and deferring – often indefinitely – the disclosure of meaning, permitting us, in the meantime, to become neither absorbed nor distracted, but, rather, implicated.

The malaise we experience during these long takes is intensified when the frame is deserted by the bodies that normally provide a stable on-screen point of identification for our gaze. In the final sequence of *La Pianiste*, the stationary camera continues to film the conservatory's façade long after Erika, wounded but resolute, has exited the building and the frame, postponing closure and leaving the expectation of presence which cinema creates in its viewers frustrated. In *Le Temps du loup*, the protagonists' bodies are sometimes too far away from the camera to be clearly visible; at other times the human form is simply absent from the landscape. Drained of colour and motion, some of these images begin to resemble black and white photographs. The deathly stillness of Haneke's uninhabited frames arouses further anxiety, particularly when the camera lingers upon them for too long, by prompting us to ponder what they have excluded. In their revelation of absence, such images bring off-screen space disruptively into play: the site of the unwitnessed catastrophe and also, of course, the origin of the observing gaze – the space we occupy as viewers.

The concluding sequence of *Le Temps du loup* invites us to reconsider the dimensions of off-screen space. As we view images of trees and scrubland from the perspective of a camera we presume must be on a train, judging by the motion and the soundtrack, the disjunction between the unpeopled wilderness and the implied presence of an onlooker provokes a series of questions. Who is looking, and when and why? Is this an image of salvation, the advent of the redemption sought by Ben as he prepares to sacrifice himself in the sequence before, or is it simply a dreamscape, a seductive but ultimately ephemeral visualisation of the family's fantasy of rescue? Haneke's refusal to illuminate the shadowlands outside the frame leaves these questions, and thus the narrative itself, undecidable.

Haunted images: *Caché*

'L'image cinématographique est hantée par ce qui ne s'y trouve pas',[14] writes Pascal Bonitzer, one of the most articulate theorists of the often-neglected space which lies outside the frame (1971–72: 16). Seeking to elucidate the relationship between this and the space on-screen, Bonitzer notes that what the image excludes or represses may return to disturb it, a disturbance that may take the form of a haunting. Haneke's images might be viewed as 'haunted' in this sense on the many occasions when their *mise en scène* and sound refocus attention on ominous presences lurking beyond the frame. Off-screen space is regularly the site of bodily violence and catastrophe in his films. Ironic in view of the criticisms levelled at films such as *Benny's Video* and *Funny Games* on the grounds of their 'excessive' violence is the fact that this violence largely takes place unwitnessed; what we see instead are its traumatic after-effects. Also perplexing from this perspective are some of the parallels that have been drawn between *La Pianiste* and the recent trend in French cinema for sexually explicit and often graphically violent fictions, a trend epitomised by Catherine Breillat's *Romance* (1999) and Virginie Despentes's and Coralie Trinh Thi's *Baise-moi* (2000) (see, for example, Metelmann 2003: 270).[15] Emphatically disputing such parallels, and citing instead the influence of Pier Paolo Pasolini's *Salò* (1975) and Nagisa Oshima's *In the Realm of the Senses* (1976), Haneke asserts that the task he set himself on this occasion was to make an 'obscene' film without making a 'pornographic' one, in line with his reading of Jelinek's text (2001a: 191). In contrast to *Romance* and *Baise-moi*, *La Pianiste* carefully avoids images of genitalia, cutting away from these body parts and focusing on others during acts of fellatio, intercourse and self-harm.

However, the dispatch of violent and sexual acts to off-screen space neither sanitises the images nor puts the audience at their ease. Noting that the unimaged torture in *Funny Games* is represented in real time on the soundtrack, Philippe Rouyer observes that Haneke's

14 'The cinematic image is haunted by what isn't there'.

15 More persuasive in this context are the parallels Sharrett draws between *La Pianiste* and Gaspar Noé's *Irréversible* (2002). Pointing out the films' common concern with 'patriarchal sexuality's association with the monstrous' and with the oversights and blindspots of the European intellectual tradition, he proposes that *Irréversible* might be read as an 'apocalyptic coda' to *La Pianiste* (Sharrett 2004).

'rejet de l'ellipse ... confisque au hors-champ son statut de refuge rassurant: la bande sonore oblige à imaginer ce que la caméra refuse de montrer' (1998: 37).[16] The same is true of the murder scene in *Benny's Video*, which we view re-mediated on Benny's video monitor. Although his victim drops to the floor and out of both the cinematic and the video frame the instant he shoots her, her cries and groans supply an aural witness to the death throes taking place largely beyond these frames. The 'obscenity' of such images, their capacity to disturb rather than console, resides in the charged relation between what we see and what remains hidden. According to Haneke, it is the excessive visibility cultivated by pornography, rather than the recourse to off-screen space, that affords catharsis in its endeavour 'to render the obscene consumable, saleable' (2001a: 191). In this account, pornography becomes an attempt to 'bandage ... our social and psychological wound' (a palliative function which Haneke also attributes to propaganda films) (2003: 31).

Mattias Frey (2003) has proposed a series of suggestive connections between Haneke's refusal to accord us visual access to the violent event and certain currents in trauma theory, in particular debates around the *Bilderverbot* often erroneously associated with Claude Lanzmann's landmark meditation on the legacy of the Nazi death camps, *Shoah* (1985). While Lanzmann dismisses his critics' claims that he has pronounced interdictions or taboos on atrocity images (2000: 14–15), his consistent withdrawal, in *Shoah*, from the consolatory space of representation attests to an ethical intuition that direct images of violence can conceal as much as they reveal, a suspicion shared by Haneke. It is revealing in this context that both cite what they view as the dangerously sensational, spectacular violence in Steven Spielberg's controversial *Schindler's List* (1993) as epitomising what Haneke would call the 'pornography' and Lanzmann the 'obscenity' of dominant representational forms (Haneke 2001b; Lanzmann 1994).

As its title suggests, Haneke's most recent film, *Caché*, remaps off-screen space in newly provocative ways, impregnating it with privileged meaning and an unprecedented density of presence. Both Bonitzer's spectral metaphor and Lanzmann's qualms about the direct representation of violence are particularly resonant in the context of

16 'rejection of ellipses ... divests off-screen space of its status as a reassuring refuge: the sound-track compels us to imagine what the camera refuses to show'.

Haneke's first foray into the realm of historical trauma and personal and collective memory. On 17 October 1961, originally peaceful pro-FLN (Front de Libération Nationale) demonstrations on the streets of Paris culminated in an unprovoked massacre of unarmed Algerians by the French police, the facts of which were largely silenced by the authorities and the media at the time. *Caché*'s images are haunted by the memory of this atrocity and the media's role in its repression, as the victims' ghosts return to survey the living from off-screen space – and to hold them to account.

The film is framed by two characteristically protracted stationary real-time takes, which show, as the opening and closing credits roll respectively, the façade of a house in a peaceful Parisian street and students milling around outside the entrance to a school. As the seconds and then minutes slip by, the ostensible banality of these images, which initially appear devoid of narratively significant action or even a clearly signalled focus of attention, begins to unsettle the audience. Our attention wanders instead to off-screen space, as we wonder who is filming these images and why. The absence of a counter-shot disrupts the mechanisms through which cinema habitually sutures its spectators seamlessly into its diegetic fictions, preventing us from making sense of the space outside the frame.[17] In the opening sequence, anxious voices eventually intrude on the soundtrack and tracking marks appear on the surface of the images as they suddenly accelerate, as if someone has pressed the fast-forward button on a remote control. These aural and visual clues identify the images as belonging to a videotape sent anonymously to the family living in the house surveyed. Spatial relations are reconfigured as we realise we are not outside but inside the house viewing the tape with its addressees. As the film unfolds, however, the origin of the tapes remains enigmatic and the presence behind the video-camera remains hidden; his or her identity and motives remain the missing pieces in the intricate narrative puzzle.

Caché maps the grey zones of individual and collective guilt and responsibility laid bare when the padded bourgeois cocoon inhabited by Georges, Anne and Pierrot is ruptured by a concerted campaign

17   I am drawing here on Jean-Pierre Oudart's seminal account of suture (1969), which identifies the shot/counter-shot system, a succession of cuts that efface their own presence, as the principal suturing device in classical narrative cinema.

of surveillance and harassment. The prime suspect is initially Majid, whose Algerian parents were employed by Georges's family but failed to return from the demonstrations of October 1961. Georges's parents decided to adopt Majid, but were persuaded to send him away by the lies of their jealous six-year-old son. Suspicion subsequently passes to Majid's (unnamed) son, yet the final sequence, depicting an inaudible conversation between him and Pierrot, leaves the matter unresolved. Those we initially presume to be innocent begin to look guiltier and those presumed guilty look more innocent under the gaze of a hidden eye which belongs to neither director nor spectator and yet which seems to appoint itself as moral authority and arbiter of justice. 'Je n'ai rien à cacher',[18] protests Georges. Yet his consistent failure to acknowledge responsibility for the past or to redeem himself through ethical action in the present begs to be read allegorically in relation not only to the troubled memory of the Franco-Algerian war and the postcolonial fracture in France, but also to every faulty or selective national memory.[19] Contemporary television coverage of the Iraqi and Israeli-Palestinian conflicts absent-mindedly viewed by Georges as he ponders his options establishes a further series of connections between distant suffering past and present, foregrounding the media's collusion in processes of collective amnesia. Television is firmly implicated here, as elsewhere in Haneke's work, in what Mary Ann Doane has described as 'the annihilation of memory, and consequently of history, in its continual stress upon the "nowness" of its own discourse' (1990: 227).

Freudian, Sartrean and Foucauldian discourses thus compete in *Caché* for interpretive authority as the revenge-bent repressed returns to expose Georges's *mauvaise conscience* through a regime of punitive surveillance. So who is filming? This vexed issue is further obfuscated by Haneke's decision to shoot the whole film in high definition digital video and by the preponderance of static sequence shots. The formal and textural distinctions between the covertly filmed videotapes and the other images are thereby minimised; indeed, many

18 'I have nothing to hide'.
19 'On trouve ces "taches noires" d'un passé mal assumé dans l'histoire de tous les pays' ('We find the "black marks" of pasts that have not been properly accepted in the history of every country'), remarks Haneke, who argues that *Caché* works just as powerfully as an allegory of Austria's reluctance to accept responsibility for its complicity in Nazi crimes (2005b: 23).

of the latter begin to resemble surveillance footage. Gradually, then, every image becomes suspect. This is equally true of the third type of image presented by the film: shadowy fragments and then longer sequences depicting scenes from Majid's childhood trauma. These memory-images offer subjective insights of a kind rare in the work of an avowedly anti-psychological filmmaker. Until this film, Haneke has rigorously eschewed flashbacks on the grounds that they are liable to assume an explanatory function which oversimplifies reality (whence his excision, in *La Pianiste*, of the flashbacks in Jelinek's novel) (see Haneke and Jelinek 2001: 96). Since the trauma scenes in *Caché* resurface in Georges's guilt-ridden memory and haunted nightmares, they remain unreliable witnesses which question memory's relationship to history.

The difficulty of determining the status and origins of any given sequence in the film places spectators and protagonists in parallel predicaments and, like Georges and Anne, we begin to feel increasingly paranoid. In *Caché* the video apparatus itself colludes in the practices of deception, illusion and betrayal that drive the narrative. Like the hidden filmmaker who manipulates the fiction, Haneke is playing knowing games with his viewers, reminiscent of the ludic ploys in *Code inconnu*, where the distinction between different layers of reality is repeatedly obscured, and in *Funny Games*, where the serial killers are able to rewind and replay the action at whim. Haneke's films persistently call into question the ontological status of their images, testing their power to sustain illusions and exploiting the viewer's desire to be deceived. These coercive tactics are ostensibly unconducive to the process of dialogue which the director claims he aims to open between film and spectators, suggesting that his pledged dedication to 'interactivity' cannot be taken at face value.

With the notable exception of the chilling images of Majid slitting his throat, which we view as they are filmed, we view the anonymous videotapes in *Caché* on a television screen as they are watched by Georges and Anne, rather than through the lens of the camera as they are recorded.[20] Our viewing position thus coincides not only with that of the menacing presence behind the video-camera but also with those of the terrorised couple as they replay, accelerate, rewind and freeze the tapes, deforming, reorganising and remaking the images

20 Peucker makes this point in relation to the video images in *Benny's Video* in an illuminating essay on the 'Vergletscherungs-Trilogie' (2000: 182).

as they scan them for clues to the identity of their persecutor. In the era of digital video and remote controls, viewers too can manipulate images and interact with them in multifarious ways. Spectatorship is dramatised in Haneke's films as a potentially transforming and transformative experience, and, above all, as a heterogeneous one, by turns passive and hands-on, compliant and resistant, distanced and intimate. While visual pleasures remain suspect or elusive, viewing positions and identifications prove fluid, plural and contradictory. Haneke's manipulative images do not preclude resistant readings but can empower us to participate in interactive processes of sense-making. Doubt, suspicion and deception are part and parcel of this ethical encounter. After all, as Haneke likes to claim, paraphrasing Jean-Luc Godard's famous Bazinian affirmation of cinema's transparency 'le cinéma, c'est vingt-quatre mensonges par seconde' (in Haneke and Jelinek 2001: 99).[21]

Through this playful cinephilic allusion Haneke at once aligns himself with a distinctively French tradition of authorship and parodically marks his distance from it, simultaneously claiming and cutting himself loose from a history. His French-language films highlight the instability of inherited concepts of authorship and national identity at a time when the migration of people and the circulation of images are refocusing attention on the transnational and the global. The migratory trajectories of his project remap the boundaries between nationally-specific film cultures and associated critical discourses, revealing them to be more porous than is often assumed. Haneke's unique contribution to the 'new European art cinema' described by Combs lies not only in his caustic critique of the globalised mass media and image industries but also in his incessant probing of their radical impact upon intercultural, interpersonal and familial bonds. *Code inconnu, La Pianiste, Le Temps du loup* and *Caché* trace the ways in which these bonds are threatened and reshaped by encounters with distant suffering and shared experiences of displacement, loss and mourning. Ethical meaning in Haneke's films emerges not only in their traumatic confrontations with the other's vulnerability and pain, but also, and perhaps most urgently, in their appeal to us to contemplate our own roles in these close encounters as consumers, observers, witnesses and potential actors.

21 'cinema lies twenty-four times a second'.

References

Arthur, Paul (2005), 'Endgame', *Film Comment*, 41:6 (November–December), 24–8.

Bauman, Zygmunt (2003), *Liquid Love: On the Frailty of Human Bonds*, Cambridge, Polity.

Bazin, André (1958), 'L'évolution du langage cinématographique', in *Qu'est-ce que le cinéma?*, vol. 1 'Ontologie et langage', iv vols, Paris, Cerf, 131–48.

Boltanski, Luc (1993), *La Souffrance à distance: morale humanitaire, médias et politique*, Paris, Métailié.

Bonitzer, Pascal (1971–72), 'Hors-champ (un espace en défaut)', *Cahiers du cinéma*, 234–5 (December–January–February), 15–26.

Champagne, John (2002), 'Undoing Oedipus: feminism and Michael Haneke's *The Piano Teacher*', *Bright Lights Film Journal*, 36 (April), www.brightlights-film.com/36/pianoteacher1.html, accessed 01/08/2005.

Combs, Richard (2002), 'Living in never-never land', *Film Comment*, 38:2 (March–April), 26–8.

Daney, Serge (1991), *Devant la recrudescence des vols de sacs à main: cinéma, télévision, information*, Lyon, Aléas.

Delahaye, Luc (1999), *L'Autre*, London, Phaidon.

Doane, Mary Ann (1990), 'Information, crisis, catastrophe', in Patricia Mellencamp (ed.), *Logics of Television: Essays in Cultural Criticism*, Indianapolis, Indiana University Press, pp. 222–39.

Frey, Mattias (2003), 'Michael Haneke', *Senses of Cinema*, www.sensesofcinema.com/contents/directors/03/haneke.html, accessed 03/05/2004.

Goudet, Stéphane (2000), '*Code inconnu*: la main tendue', *Positif*, 478 (December), 23–4.

Grisseman, Stefan (2001), 'In zwei, drei feinen Linien die Badewannenwand entlang. Kunst, Utopie und Selbstbeschmutzung: zu Michael Hanekes Jelinek-Adaptation', in Michael Haneke, Elfriede Jelinek and Grissemann (ed.), *Die Klavierspielerin: Drehbuch, Gespräche, Essays*, Vienna, Sonderzahl, 11–31.

Haneke, Michael (1992), 'Film als Katharsis', in Francesco Bono (ed.), *Austria (in)felix: zum österreichischem Film der 80er Jahre*, Graz, Blimp, 89.

Haneke, Michael (1996), 'Der Name der Erbsünde ist Verdrängung', in Franz Grabner, Gerhard Larcher and Christian Wessely (eds), *Utopie und Fragment: Michael Hanekes Filmwerk*, Thaur, Kulturverlag, 9–18.

Haneke, Michael (2000a), '*71 Fragments of a Chronology of Chance*: notes to the film', in Willy Riemer (ed.), *After Postmodernism: Austrian Literature and Film in Transition*, Riverside, CA, Ariadne, pp. 171–5.

Haneke, Michael (2000b), 'Beyond mainstream film', in Willy Riemer (ed.), *After Postmodernism: Austrian Literature and Film in Transition*, Riverside, CA, Ariadne, pp. 159–70.

Haneke, Michael (2000c), 'La fragmentation du regard', *Positif*, 478 (December), 25–9.

Haneke, Michael (2001a), '... einen Film zu drehen, der zugleich komisch und scheußlich ist ...', in Haneke, Elfriede Jelinek and Stefan Grissemann (ed.),

Die Klavierspielerin: Drehbuch, Gespräche, Essays, Vienna, Sonderzahl, pp. 175–91.

Haneke, Michael (2001b), 'The bearded prophet of *Code inconnu* and *The Piano Teacher*', www.indiewire.com/people/int_Haneke_Michael_011204.html, accessed 03/05/2004.

Haneke, Michael (2003), 'The world that is known', *Cineaste*, 28:3 (Summer), 28–31.

Haneke, Michael (2005a), 'Nous baignons dans la culture de la culpabilité', *Télérama* (5 October).

Haneke, Michael (2005b), 'Dès qu'on pose une caméra quelque part, on manipule', *La Croix* (5 October), 23.

Haneke, Michael and Elfriede Jelinek (2001), 'Désaccords mineurs pour piano forte', *L'Avant-scène du cinéma*, 504 (September), 95–102.

Hartman, Geoffrey (2000), 'Memory.com: tele-suffering and testimony in the dot com era', *Raritan*, 19 (Winter), 1–18.

Hutchison, Nina (2003), 'Between action and repression: *The Piano Teacher*', *Senses of Cinema*, 26 (May–June), www.sensesofcinema.com/contents/03/26/piano_teacher.html, accessed 03/08/2005.

Jelinek, Elfriede (1983), *Die Klavierspielerin*, Hamburg, Rowohlt.

Lanzmann, Claude (1994), 'Holocauste, la représentation impossible', *Le Monde (Supplément Arts–Spectacles)* (3 March), i, vii.

Lanzmann, Claude (2000), 'Parler pour les morts', *Le Monde des débats* (May), 14–16.

Metelmann, Jörg (2003), *Zur Kritik der Kino-Gewalt. Die Filme von Michael Haneke*, Munich, Wilhelm Fink.

Oudart, Jean-Pierre (1969), 'La Suture' and 'La Suture (2)', *Cahiers du cinéma*, 211 and 212 (April and May), 36–9, 50–5.

Peucker, Brigitte (2000), 'Fragmentation and the real: Michael Haneke's family trilogy', in Willy Riemer (ed.), *After Postmodernism: Austrian Literature and Film in Transition*, Riverside, CA, Ariadne, pp. 176–88.

Rouyer, Philippe (1998), '*Funny Games*: souffrir n'est pas jouer', *Positif*, 443 (January), 37–8.

Sharrett, Christopher (2002), '*The Piano Teacher*', *Cineaste*, 27:4 (Fall), 37–40.

Sharrett, Christopher (2004), 'The horror of the middle class: Michael Haneke's *La Pianiste*', *Kinoeye*, 4:1 (March), www.kinoeye.org/04/01/sharrett01.php, accessed 02/09/2005.

Sontag, Susan (2003), *Regarding the Pain of Others*, New York, Farrar, Straus and Giroux.

Williams, Linda (1989), *Hard Core: Power, Pleasure, and the 'Frenzy of the Visible'*, Berkeley, University of California Press.

Wood, Robin (2002), '"Do I disgust you?" Or, tirez pas sur *La Pianiste*', *CineAction*, 59 (September), 54–61.

Žižek, Slavoj (1999), *The Ticklish Subject: The Absent Centre of Political Ontology*, London, Verso.

5

François Ozon's cinema of desire

Kate Ince

By the age of thirty-seven François Ozon had seven features and a
clutch of admired short films to his credit. But in France, his reputation has taken a very different course from the one it is now starting
to get from Anglophone critics, whose familiarity with (or at least
exposure to) the academic discourses of cultural studies, gender and
queer theory attunes them to the centrality of sexuality to Ozon's
oeuvre. Ozon's films to date have oscillated between the exuberant and
satirical send-ups of bourgeois family life *Sitcom* (1998) and *8 Femmes*
(*8 Women*, 2001), and the contrastingly sober *Sous le sable* (*Under the
Sand*, 2000) and *5 x 2* (2004), both of which address that staple theme
of French drama 'le couple' – an oscillation that sets Ozon apart from
the kind of stylistic unity usually associated with being an *auteur*, and
has made it possible for some critics to polarise his output and make
some damagingly judgemental dismissals of key elements of what
I am calling his 'cinema of desire'. Frédéric Bonnaud, for example,
has progressively reviewed the feature films for the Parisian culture
magazine *Les Inrockuptibles*, and in 2001, after the international release
of *Sous le sable*, saw his overview of Ozon's work to date translated for
the leading American journal *Film Comment*, under the title 'François
Ozon: wannabe *auteur* makes good'.[1] The very title of this article
reveals Bonnaud assessing Ozon against a maturational framework
that represents the most conventional and limiting kind of auteurism:
Bonnaud claims that in *Sous le sable*, Ozon has successfully adopted
a 'calmer, more suggestive, unforced approach' in comparison to his
previous 'youthful efforts', and finally 'found his voice' (Bonnaud

1 The piece was published in French in *Les Inrockuptibles* No. 324, pp. 28–31.

2001: 55), and goes on to set up a Manichaean opposition between Ozon's 'youthful' and 'mature' filmmaking. One particular shot of *Regarde la mer* (*See the sea*, 1997) – the protagonist brushing her teeth with a toothbrush that has recently been dipped in a toilet bowl of excrement – is accused of crudity, heavy-handedness and a 'terrible lapse in taste' (I shall show later how Ozon's 'tasteless' interest in dirt and excessive, farcically performed sexual scenarios are essential parts of his filmic universe), and in *Sitcom* Bonnaud finds 'shameless caricature', 'shock value' and 'frantically and indiscriminately piled up' comic effects (Bonnaud 2001: 54). In addressing Ozon's *oeuvre* up to *5 x 2* in this chapter, one of my aims is to show that the condemnation of Ozon's 'immaturity' typified by Bonnaud's criticism[2] has served to mask the depth and brilliance of Ozon's exploration of sexuality, and his originality as France's first mainstream queer *auteur*.

During the 1990s, Ozon was remarked upon as an obviously 'gay' filmmaker. But although he can be seen as the most recent addition to a trend in French cinema that 'suggests sexual fluidity in new, innovative ways',[3] Ozon's films distinguish themselves clearly from earlier gay male filmic production in France through never having gay communities as their social setting, through their absence of reference to SIDA (AIDS), and through never having overtly politicised narratives. Ozon is linked just as significantly to cinematic traditions, French and international, by the homage to Rainer Werner Fassbinder constituted by his filming of a Fassbinder play in *Gouttes d'eau sur pierres brûlantes* (*Water Drops on Burning Rocks*, 1999), and by the 'Buñuelian' subversiveness of *Sitcom* and *8 Femmes*, films which, as Jonathan Romney observes, represent a singular queering of the tradition of surrealist subversion of the bourgeoisie (Romney 1999: 56).

In *Une robe d'été* (*Summer Dress*, 1996), the first of Ozon's shorts to meet with critical acclaim, a young man on holiday with his boyfriend is irritated by the latter's singing and dancing along to a song by French pop icon Sheila. The young man, Sébastien, rides his bike to the beach, where a young Spanish woman, Lucia, having introduced herself by asking for a light, invites him to go and have sex in

2 As Andrew Asibong states, it has become 'the prevailing view' that 'Ozon's ongoing obsession with transgression ... has fortunately given way to allegedly more mature projects' (Asibong 2005: 203).

3 Schilt suggests that André Téchiné can be regarded as a precursor of this tendency, and lists a number of other key works that make it up (Schilt 2004: 1).

the woods. When he returns to the beach, Sébastien finds his clothes have been stolen, and is forced to cycle home wearing a dress lent to him by Lucia. But after initially feeling self-conscious about this, he starts to enjoy it, and when he gets home, his feminine appearance turns out to be a turn-on for his boyfriend, leading to vigorous sex in which the dress gets ripped. He sews up the tear and later returns it to Lucia, who does not want it back, and tells him 'Je te l'offre, elle peut te servir'.[4]

As Thibaut Schilt points out, the fluidity of sexual orientation dramatised in *Une robe d'été* is coterminous with gender identity (Schilt 2004: 2): it is the feminine appearance of the dress that arouses the desire of the gay boyfriend. Ozon is not so much working with the Freudian understanding of 'masculine' as 'active' and 'feminine' as 'passive' – although this applies to the gay couple's sex – as suggesting that sexual orientation is only ever 'fixed' in the most provisional manner: in the course of a day, Sébastien goes from 'gay', to 'straight', to 'gay' again. In addition to lending the light-heartedness and summery guilt-free atmosphere to *Une robe d'été* that makes it so appealing, this provisionality of sexual orientation chimes with Judith Butler's theory of gender performativity, according to which sex acts, like speech acts and acts of dressing, contribute to a non-binary understanding of gender identity that includes gays, lesbians, and bi- and transsexuals. Initially set out in her 1990 book *Gender Trouble: Feminism and the Subversion of Identity*, which became one of the founding texts of queer theory, Butler's theory of gender performativity has now been augmented by the writings of a host of other theorists and critics, some of whom focus explicitly on queer desire.

This introduction to Ozon's films will revolve around the centrality of queer desire to his cinema, and the continual performative trans-formations of identity worked within it. Butler's deconstruction, in *Gender Trouble*, of what she calls the 'heterosexual matrix', exposed the thoroughgoing social normativity of compulsory heterosexuality: as Tim Dean puts it, '"queer" came to stand less for a particular sexual orientation of a stigmatized erotic identity than for a critical distance from the white, middle-class, heterosexual norm' (Dean 2003: 240). 'Gay' often simply opposes straight, and 'queer' is not just an umbrella

4 'Keep it, it might come in useful'.

term for 'gay, lesbian and bisexual': it 'sets itself more broadly in opposition to the forces of normalization that regulate social conformity'
(Dean 2003: 240). In so doing, queer texts and films constitute a privileged site for the imagination and *mise en scène* of new social formations – the kind of 'new relational modes' envisaged by Leo Bersani
and Ulysse Dutoit in their reading of Pedro Almodóvar's *All About My
Mother* (1999) (Bersani and Dutoit 2004: 103). There is a compelling
parallel to be drawn between the strand of sober, melancholy (melo)
drama that has developed in Ozon's work and Almodóvar's *Live Flesh*
(1997), *All About My Mother* and *Talk to Her* (2002). The emergence of
new modes of relating from the social effects of non-normative queer
sexualities is an issue I shall return to throughout this chapter. First,
however, the performativity of sexuality and identity that characterises
many of Ozon's films needs to be illustrated, and to do this, I turn to
his early set of shorts from 1998, *Scènes de lit* (*Bed Scenes*).

Performative couples

Six of the *Scènes de lit* feature heterosexual couples, compared to only
two – *L'Homme idéal* (*The Ideal Man*) and *Les Puceaux* (*The Virgins*) –
whose pairings are homosexual. Irony and the humour of apparent
compatibility that turns sour are to the fore in *M. Propre* (*Mr Clean*),[5]
whose male protagonist is a sort of anti-capitalist contemporary hippie
opposed to all but the most necessary washing – of his body, his clothes
or his living space. As he expounds this philosophy to his bed-partner
she grows increasingly uneasy, then gets up and leaves, announcing
that she has been an asthma sufferer since childhood. Incompatibility
is also only discovered between the sheets in *L'Amour dans le noir* (*Love
in the Dark*), where Frank is unable to have sex with Virginie with the
light on, against gender stereotyping according to her. She refuses to
comply in the dark but, since he becomes aroused as soon as the light
is off, gives in to his request to be allowed to masturbate at her side.
His satisfaction at this heals their rift and re-establishes tenderness as
they wish each other goodnight (they are obliged to spend the night
together, since Virginie has missed the last métro home). The third

5 Or *Mr Sheen*, since *M. Propre* is also the brand name of the French equivalent of
   this cleaning product, an ironic dig at capitalist consumerism clearly intended
   in Ozon's title.

potentially mismatched pairing of the set of films is between a fifty-two-year-old woman and a nineteen-year-old boy in *Madame*: despite the woman's reticence about beginning the first sexual relationship she will have had since the death of her husband five years earlier, her refusal meets with unlikely tenacity and patience from her young partner, which then turns into a kind of courtly love shivering with eroticism, as he asks simply to be allowed to kiss her hand. Meanwhile, *Tête bêche (Heads or Tails)*, the fourth scene of the set, is unlike any of the others in featuring lovers who seem already to be an established couple (in it, foreplay consists of counting down from 100 to 69). But it turns around a number and the idea of counting in a manner that reveals the preoccupation with permutations and permutability latent in all Ozon's dramas about couples. *Scènes de lit* as a whole, whether or not it is regarded as a unified entity, has the structure of a catalogue or instructive illustration.

It is in the two scenes of the set about same-sex pairings that the space of mutable sexuality established in *Une robe d'été* of two years earlier is most clearly to the fore. The two young men of *Les Puceaux* have qualified and opposing claims to virginal status: one of them has never had sex with women, the other never with men. Any stereotypical representation of gay male sex is renounced as the two modestly opt for a kiss as the best expression of their feelings for each other. In *L'Homme idéal*, meanwhile, Ozon captures the psychic mechanism of idealisation brilliantly, as one woman takes advantage of another's vulnerable projection onto a man she has flirted with in order to declare her love for her friend (and get it reciprocated), by 'therapeutically' standing in for the wished-for male lover. In the realm of fantasy and projection, sexual/gender difference is of no consequence, and sexual orientation and identity are in sway to a love composed as much of affection and a wish to comfort as of bodily desire.

Perhaps Ozon's most extended illustration of a change of lovers that is also a shift from a heterosexual to a homosexual orientation occurs to Luc, in *Les Amants criminels (Criminal Lovers*, 1998). After the murder of their schoolfellow Saïd to which Alice has incited Luc, and their subsequent flight from home, the lovers are imprisoned by a woodsman,[6] who has seen them bury (and who then digs up) Saïd's body, and has decided to take advantage of the criminality he has

6 'l'homme des bois'.

witnessed. While Alice is locked in the earthen cellar of his hut with Saïd's body and starved of food and drink, Luc is shackled but also fed chunks of meat by the woodsman, who explains, albeit enigmatically, that he likes girls just to be well-muscled, but prefers his boys 'bien dodus'.[7] As Luc lies next to him on his iron-framed bed, the woodsman unzips the top layers of his clothes and starts to masturbate him, Luc's breathing indicating that this gives him pleasure. Later that night, when Luc is interned in the cellar for having started to follow Alice's instructions to kill the sleeping woodsman with a kitchen knife, he is unable to acknowledge to her the satisfaction at the orgasm he has had. Later still, he is hauled back upstairs for full intercourse, which evidently also satisfies him. Although Luc nonetheless takes the opportunity presented to him shortly afterwards to 'escape' from the hut with Alice (to certain further confinement, since the police have had time to track the pair down), he reveals his attachment to their jailer by shouting 'Laissez-le!'[8] repeatedly to the police, as they arrest and brutally kick his first male lover. *Les Amants criminels* was much criticised on its release (Schilt calls the woodsman 'paedophile' (Schilt 2004: 4)), and it is hard to avoid concluding that this is because of its illustration of the inextricable relationship of sex and power: without his enforced confinement and separation from Alice, Luc would not have discovered his primary sexual orientation.

Both *Les Amants criminels* and the eight miniatures that make up the *Scènes de lit* show Ozon ringing the changes on the forms of the couple, dramatising trajectories of erotic desire that prove amusing or touching, while indicating, most strongly in *L'Homme idéal*, the performativity of sexual orientation. In Ozon's other feature films, fluidity of orientation is also to the fore in *Gouttes d'eau sur pierres brûlantes*, in the characters of Léopold and Franz, who have respectively lived and been drawn to a life of normative heterosexuality, but not been defined by it, Léopold in repeated relationships with younger men, Franz in meeting Léopold. An adaptation of a play by Fassbinder, *Gouttes d'eau* is a chamber piece restricted to the four characters of Léopold, Franz, Anna (Franz's ex-girlfriend) and Véra, Léopold's ex-live-in-partner. Of the six sexual relationships that might be formed between these characters, four of them actually are. Similar multiple couplings and switches in orientation abound in *8 Femmes*, where

7 'nice and plump'.
8 'Leave him alone!'

four of the eight women are either revealed to be lesbian or bisexual or give in to non-heterosexual dallying in the course of the action. Repeatedly in Ozon's dramas, the structure of the couple, heterosexual *or* homosexual, underpins the action more firmly than does normative heterosexuality, binary sexual difference or stable sexual orientation.[9]

Queering the family

From his earliest short *Photo de famille* (*Family Photo*, 1988), the family has been central to Ozon's cinema. (And it is tempting here to change the definite article to a possessive, and say 'his family', since his parents, sister and brother are the film's cast.) Originally shot on Super-8 and without a soundtrack, *Photo de famille* gives expression to the murderous impulses latent in a middle-class, nuclear family almost casually: after finishing watching a movie together, the mother, father, son and daughter eat supper then return to their various activities. The daughter does her homework, the father dozes on the sofa; the son, however, brings fatally drugged coffee to his mother, stabs his sister with a pair of scissors, then smothers his father with a cushion. Next, he lines up the bodies on the same sofa on which they sat together to watch the movie at the start of the film, sets the self-timer on his camera, and takes the family photo of the film's title, in which his beaming smile and straight sitting posture are juxtaposed with the melodramatic grimaces and contorted bodies of his parents and sibling. (Itself an echo of a shot in Buñuel's *Le Charme discret de la bourgeoisie* (*The Discreet Charm of the Bourgeoisie*, 1972), this scene also anticipates an extremely similar one in *Sitcom* where the bodies of the mother, son and daughter, along with some of the family's hangers-on, are lined up on a sofa after being shot, in what turns out to be a fantasy on the part of the father.)

Melodrama is central to *Photo de famille*, as it will also be to *Sitcom* and *Gouttes d'eau sur pierres brûlantes*. Camerawork and shot length

9 The future towards which Ozon's films point, one might say, is a future of coupling. As Bersani and Dutoit remark of Godard's *Le Mépris* (1963), '[the kind of presence Odysseus and Penelope and *The Odyssey* have in *Contempt*] ... has nothing to do with likeness or unlikeness, but rather with the identical ontological status of both couples: that of possibility. The past, like the present, is always *waiting to be*' (Bersani and Dutoit 2004: 66).

are calculated to emphasise the drama of the unrealistically quick and efficient murders (no blood is seen when the sister is stabbed), and the son, played by Guillaume Ozon and clearly some sort of autobiographical persona for the director, exaggerates his gestures and his expressions to suit, making them resemble countless familiar moments from horror films. *Victor* (1993), another short that revolves around the central character's killing of his parents, this time seemingly an unpremeditated and desperate act (Victor has a gun in his own mouth in the first scene of the film), demonstrates the murderous violence of Oedipal relationships and their link to sexuality more explicitly: once his guilty fright over the murder has passed, Victor can masturbate, is included in foreplay and sex between the family maid Julie and her lover, and is last seen – once he has buried his parents' bodies in the garden – catching a train, presumably into the city away from the parental home, a kind of gothic *château*. He is wearing just trousers and a vest, and a jacket hangs casually over his shoulder; he looks at ease with himself and like a young man with a future, no longer the anguished youth with nowhere to turn that bourgeois family existence had reduced him to.

Ozon's blackly humorous treatment of death in both *Photo de famille* and *Victor* is potentially more interesting than the films' Oedipal narratives: bodies piled up on the sofa in *Photo de famille*, and the way Victor drags his parents' corpses around the house and garden with him, arranging them in grotesque poses, show the materiality of death helping the son to adjust to his new-found freedom, while also celebrating it. The dead father's body figures similarly in *La Petite Mort* (*Little Death*, 1995), whose protagonist Paul's damaged sense of self is at the root of his preference for having himself photographed at the moment of orgasm, and who photographs his father's corpse with power-hungry hastiness, desiring to repair the damage done to his self-esteem by the unloving parent. But if Ozon's fathers have to be murdered or their death celebrated in the early films, the death of the father at the end of *La Petite Mort* gives way to a repeated absence of father figures from no less than four of the families in the films that follow: in *Regarde la mer* Sasha's husband is away working until he returns to make the shocking discovery of her mutilated body; in *Sitcom* the father is 'absent' despite being physically present (a contradiction I shall explain); in *8 Femmes* the family patriarch is presumed dead until his actual death occurs at the end of the film, and *Swimming*

Pool (2003) uncovers the hidden past and illegitimate daughter of a London publisher who is absent from most of the action of the film, since his unacknowledged daughter lives in France, where he owns a second home.

Sitcom, the first full-length feature that gained Ozon his reputation as the new 'bad boy' (Bonnaud 2001: 54) of French cinema, does indeed play with the televisual genre of the sitcom, in its unflinching display of the private, emotional and sexual lives of a group of characters. As Schilt summarises, 'the film's intentions are clearly to subvert and transgress the norms of middle-class *bonne société*, as it explicitly presents or suggests every perversion and taboo in the book: homosexuality, interracial adultery, sadomasochism, incest, paedophilia, group sex, even bestiality' (Schilt 2004: 3). This unleashing of non-normative sexualities and desires on the family follows the father's 'adoption' as the family pet of a white laboratory rat, an act that horrifies his wife, played with brilliant deadpan humour by Evelyne Dandry, but delights his son Nicolas and daughter Sophie. The same evening, Nicolas announces to the family at dinner that he is gay, and that night, Sophie attempts suicide by jumping from an upstairs window, an 'accident' that leaves her paralysed from the waist down and transforms her into an embittered and sadistic dominatrix, confined to a wheelchair in which she is attended by boyfriend David, whose devotion to her now extends to masochistic role-play. The family home, pictured at the start of the film in exaggerated sunny suburban tranquillity complete with cuckoo, becomes the scene of orgies advertised in the local paper and held in Nicolas' room, then – finally – incest as Nicolas is seduced by his mother, desperate to reunite her disintegrating family by showing some of the love she diagnoses it as lacking.

The *dramatis personae* of both *Sitcom* and *8 Femmes* is a classically patriarchal family, in which gender roles and generational differences function according to the highly familiar dynamics of the bourgeoisie. In *Sitcom*, it is only during the therapy programme the mother attends with her children as the last resort in her effort to save family unity that she hits on the interpretation that the rat is to blame for the family's disintegration, upon which she phones her husband instructing him to kill it. The equivalence of the father to the rat is finally made explicit when, after putting it in the family's microwave then consuming its charred body, he is transformed into a giant, very un-cute version of the pet. Freud's equation of oral and cannibalistic desires to psychic identification is literalised: the father 'is' the rat, its destructive 'influence' on the family is his own, and once his wife, son and daughter have confronted and dealt with his malevolence, they can move on, living new and different lives because the dominating, restricting hold of patriarchal law over them is at an end. 'To lose ... the paternal function at once dependent upon and incommensurable with any real father, is to lose the Law that governs and stabilises the attributing of identities' (Bersani and Dutoit 2004: 103). This hold is illustrated during the film by the father's withdrawn intellectualism and complete refusal to engage with his family emotionally: when Nicolas announces he is gay, the father treats the assembled company to a lecture on homosexuality in ancient Greece, and when his wife calls the crisis meeting to suggest that they all attend a programme of therapy together, he simply shambles back to his crossword, saying it will doubtless do the three of them good, but is simply of no relevance to him.

As a vehicle for its female actresses Catherine Deneuve, Danielle Darrieux, Emmanuelle Béart, Fanny Ardant, Isabelle Huppert, Virginie Ledoyen, Ludivine Sagnier, and Firmine Richard, *8 Femmes* pays homage to and indulges its stars, offering them each a musical number in the form of a French pop single from a past decade, and decking them out in gorgeous costumes that take their inspiration from 1950s Hollywood. Ozon says of the film that 'the dress of Fanny Ardant was a reference to Ava Gardner and Cyd Cherisse. Catherine Deneuve was more Lana Turner or Marilyn Monroe', and specifies that he was seeking to revive the idea of Technicolor (Ozon 2002: 3). As Jean-Marc Lalanne summarises, 'François Ozon has made *the* most deliberately "meta" film in French cinema' (Lalanne 2002: 82), which continually references both Hollywood panache and glamour and his actresses' past performances in French films: Deneuve utters a line to Ledoyen spoken to her by one of Truffaut's male characters in both *La Sirène du Mississippi* (1969) and *Le Dernier Métro* (1980), and Darrieux and Deneuve replay an exaggerated and crueller version of the conflictual mother–daughter relationship they acted in the films of Jacques Demy (Lalanne 2002: 82). *8 Femmes* could be read, I thought when I first saw it, as an opulent and utterly knowing pastiche of 1950s French studio cinema. But if the film is a vibrant, colour-laden and highly self-conscious pastiche of the 'cinéma de papa' as this description suggests, it is not one whose plot should be dismissed as lightweight and 'transparent' (Lalanne 2002: 82). The continual far-fetched narrative twists effected by the women's divulgence of their respective relationships with the patriarch Marcel (who was husband, son-in-law, step-father, real father, brother, lover and employer to them, often playing more than one role to each woman), and the development of their relationships with each other that results from these revelations amounts to an acting-out of every possible desiring relation except male homosexuality. Chanel, the black servant, is in love with Pierrette, Marcel's bisexual sister, who rejects her for her lowly social status, but whose rivalry with Gaby, Marcel's wife, turns momentarily into a lipstick lesbian embrace in high style: meanwhile, Louise the maid is revealed to have been the lover of both her former (domestic) mistress and Marcel, and symbolically swaps her social inferiority for perverse sexual power by letting her hair down and transforming her maid's attire into a seductive 'little black dress' complete with fishnet stockings and garter. Patriarchal power, shored up by the incest taboo and the taboo against homosexuality, gives way to the sexual order that ensues when the norms of compulsory heterosexuality are comprehensively queered. But when it turns out that the entire murder plot is a charade orchestrated by the film's youngest character Catherine, Marcel's daughter, and that he is alive and well behind the locked door of his room, he shoots himself in the head anyway, unable to live with or in the new post-patriarchal regime Catherine's staging of his death has unmasked.

Unlike *Sitcom* and *8 Femmes*, *Gouttes d'eau sur pierres brûlantes* does not feature a family of characters. There are intimations of sadomasochism in the relationship between fifty-year-old worldly-wise businessman Léopold and twenty-year-old ingénue Franz, whom Léopold seduces after bringing him home to his flat, and out of the bedroom Léopold is unequivocally the dominant partner: Franz's life with him is soon nothing more than a domestic routine of cooking, cleaning and waiting for his lover to return from work. Depressed and isolated after six months of Léopold's foul-tempered egotism, Franz turns to his former girlfriend Anna when she visits to tell him another man has asked her to marry him. But Anna is drawn in by Léopold's sexual prowess just as Franz himself was (Léopold admitted his bisexuality to Franz at the outset of their relationship, stating that he had previously lived with a woman for seven years, but 'preferred boys'), and Franz takes poison, reduced to suicidal despair by Léopold's obliviousness to his love. As he lies dying, Franz is attended only by Véra, Léopold's former partner, whom we learn is a male-to-female transsexual who became a woman just in order to please Léopold, and has been unable to free herself from the orbit of Léopold's desire. But although *Gouttes d'eau* does not feature a family of characters, Léopold might be considered a kind of father-figure in the drama: he is a generation older than Franz and Anna, and his seduction of Franz is a response to the fantasy of seduction by a father-figure Franz has just narrated to him. If Léopold's status as father-figure is acknowledged, then dominant, egotistic, malevolent *paternal* sexuality becomes the motor force and dramatic atmosphere of the film, and the desire that drives it to its tragic conclusion.

As a result of their settings in middle-class *bonne société* and the *haute bourgeoisie* respectively, and their high degree of theatricality, these three films have been assumed to lack any dimension of critique.[10] But it is precisely in their theatricality that *Sitcom, 8 Femmes* and *Gouttes d'eau* do contain a critique of patriarchy. The first two films are comic, the third is tragic, resulting in repetition and a reinforcement of the *status quo*. 'The symbolic [symbolic law] cannot be *seriously* contested' (Bersani and Dutoit 2004: 104): it is in and with comedy that Ozon goes the furthest towards showing new 'modes of relation', new social formations. The interest for women and queers of all kinds of Ozon's opening up of the family is clear, and its potential exciting.

Transformative spaces: at home and on the beach

Throughout Ozon's films to date, two spaces form the scene of the action with particular frequency: one is the home or domestic interior, the other is the beach. In *Sitcom, Gouttes d'eau sur pierres brûlantes* and *8 Femmes*, the home becomes a stage on which personal and family melodramas are played out. Theatricality characterises all three films and marks the genesis of two of them:[11] the rule of unity of place

10 Bingham terms *8 Femmes* 'Ozon's most glossy, shallow and inconsequential film to date' (Bingham 2003: 6).
11 *Gouttes d'eau* adapts Fassbinder's play of the same name, *Tropfen auf heisse Steine* (1964/65), and *8 Femmes* is loosely based on an insignificant boulevard play by a dramatist called Robert Thomas.

applies completely to *Gouttes d'eau* and *8 Femmes*, and to very nearly the whole of *Sitcom*.

Turning first to *Gouttes d'eau*, it is soon evident that Ozon is putting this containment within domestic space to meaningful use. As Adam Bingham notes, 'A recurrent composition in the film has characters seen through apartment windows from the outside with the camera looking in. It is a common Sirkian motif that suggests entrapment, as well as connoting distance when Franz and Léopold are seen in separate windows' (Bingham 2003: 4–5). The camera's remove to a position outside the apartment first occurs as Franz, forcefully encouraged by Léopold in the prelude to his seduction, tells Léopold of his brushes with homosexuality at boarding school and his fantasy about being 'entered like a girl' by an imaginary step-father with muscled legs and a hairy chest. It occurs again in daylight and driving rain, at a typical moment in the boredom Franz experiences from Monday to Friday when Léopold is away doing his job as a salesman, a third time as Franz starts to seduce Anna by imitatively repeating the same routine of seduction Léopold used on him, and a final time at the very end of the film, as Véra tries but fails to open the middle window of the three, and the camera recedes into the darkness outside as she scrabbles helplessly for air and freedom from the imprisonment to which she has voluntarily returned. The entrapment communicated by the shot is Franz's, Anna's and Véra's entrapment in Léopold's domestic space, which is not literal (Franz must have left the apartment in order to carry out his duties as 'housewife', and we are told at one point that he has had a part-time job, although none of these activities occur in filmic space), but equates to the passive and dominated role they all play in relation to Léopold. As the *Cahiers du cinéma* review observed, '[Theatre] is the ideal device to express these amorous dynamics – the power- and game-playing, the domination and submission, the seductive flattery and the betrayed abandon' (Higuinen 2000: 40). Concomitantly, it is the theatrical containment of filmic space to the domestic interior – Ozon's use of the principle of unity of place in his film – that makes that space into the 'space' of sexuality, a pre-eminently queer space in view of Léopold's and Franz's bisexuality and Véra's transsexual transformation from man to woman.

In *Sitcom*, the action never leaves the family home except in a brief shot of a swimming pool where the mother, Nicolas and Sophie swim in reinvigorating harmony as part of the family therapy programme she has brought them on, and in the final, funeral scene for the *pater familias*. The near-total confinement of the film's action to the set that is the home means that, as in *Gouttes d'eau*, domestic space contains sexualities and desires: it *is* the scene of sexuality, straight, gay, sadomasochistic and incestuous. In *Sitcom*, however, the violent (if silent) paternal rule over the home that equates it with the space of patriarchy is in terminal comic crisis. Although the location of the final scene is dictated by the film's narrative, it is also significant that the action shifts at this point from highly theatricalised cinema to a naturalistic, open-air location – a graveyard, but a sunny one. The dramatic and blackly comic excesses of *Sitcom* are also marked as parodic by the opening shot of the film, a lavish red theatre curtain that goes up on the action, revealing the bourgeois family home as the stage Ozon makes it into.

Unity of place reigns entirely supreme again in *8 Femmes*, whose origins in a boulevard play Ozon describes as a positive advantage rather than a problem ('The story had a theatrical style, and that was something I wanted to keep' (Ozon 2002: 3)). As the film's Christmas-time murder mystery builds up around the death of the family patriarch (what drew Ozon to the play's narrative was that 'it put eight women together in the same place, where one man has been killed. Within that structure, I knew I'd be able to put in my observations about women, family, and so on' (Ozon 2002: 3)), attention is repeatedly drawn to the restriction and enclosure of the action. Catherine Deneuve's character Gaby remarks that the deepening snow means they are effectively 'in Siberia, cut off from the world', and shortly afterwards it is discovered that wires have been cut that render the phone and the car unusable. The set for most of the film's action is the grand and spacious living area that forms the figurative and literal centre of the country mansion, from the back of which a grand red-carpeted staircase sweeps up past the patriarch's room, located on a sort of mezzanine level, to the women's rooms. Although some scenes are filmed in these rooms and in the kitchen, the central hallway constitutes the principal stage, from and onto which exits and entrances are made. Characters are confined to the house and its grounds: although some of the women exit from the hallway-stage, nobody succeeds in leaving the estate at any point in the film.

If the equivalence of domestic to 'sexual' space demonstrated in *Gouttes d'eau* is extended to *Sitcom* and *8 Femmes*, it becomes clear that by containing the action of his two most 'taboo-busting' comedies (Romney 1999: 56) in a newly – or differently – theatricalised bourgeois interior, Ozon achieves a focus on the home that politicises otherwise chaotically subversive material. A tragic prison in *Gouttes d'eau*, because of Ozon's fidelity to Fassbinder's original plot, the home in *Sitcom* and *8 Femmes* becomes a place open to a radical transformation of patriarchy, a queer and unpredictable space that invites new and unspecified social formations.

Although none of Ozon's films privileges the beach as a location to the same extent that *Gouttes d'eau*, *Sitcom* and *8 Femmes* do the family home, a beach is an important locus of the drama in *Une robe d'été*, *Regarde la mer*, *Sous le sable* and *5 x 2*. In *Une robe d'été*, it is both the place where Sébastien is seduced, and the place from which his clothes are stolen while he and Lucia have sex in the woods. The theft of his usual clothes equates to the 'theft' of his habitual masculine identity, and in this way equates to his first heterosexual seduction. This exactly parallels what happens to Sasha in *Regarde la mer*, when, missing sex during her husband's absence, she wanders into the woods in search of substitute pleasure with one of the gay men she and Tatiana, the *routarde* who is helping her to look after her baby, have seen cruising there. (In an earlier scene on the beach, Sasha tries in vain to find some time for a different kind of pleasure, reading, but is prevented by her toddler's need for attention.) In both films, sex on – or near – the beach is with a non-habitual partner, and involves a mismatch of sexual orientation. The beach, in other words, figures a space of liminality in these two films: it is the zone in which the fluidity or flexibility of sexual identity that applies to so many of Ozon's characters is exercised, a place of experimentation and of play.

A similar observation can be made of *Sous le sable*, although the shift in identity to which Marie is subjected on the beach is primarily psychic and social. For her, the beach is a site of loss, even of trauma, since within the space of the hour in which her husband disappears, apparently into the sea, she ceases to be the devoted wife who has returned to this place with her husband year after year, and enters a period of loss and melancholia from which she does not recover in the time-frame of the film. When she returns to their seaside home much later, to identify what may well be her husband's body, finally recovered from the sea, she refuses to recognise as his the personal effects found with it. She then walks to the beach, where she sits on the sand

and sobs openly, before spotting a man standing some distance away towards whom she runs, still vainly searching for Jean, hoping that he is alive. Marie's loss of her habitual identity seems to be enduring, and is symptomatised in melancholic denial, imagined visions of her vanished husband that are shared with the viewer of *Sous le sable* to such unusual dramatic effect.

The arrestingly beautiful image from *5 x 2* posted on Ozon's website before the film's French release in September 2004, of its protagonists Gilles and Marion walking down a Sardinian beach to take a first swim in the sea together, ensures that the beach is a significant location in the film. It is unpopulated, though presumably only a short distance from the holiday camp where Gilles, vacationing with his partner Valérie, and Marion, who has come to the resort alone after a female friend has let her down at the last minute, re-encounter one another (they work for the same company, but are only slightly acquainted). After dinner *à trois* the previous evening, followed by a resort entertainment in which Gilles, seemingly uncharacteristically, has made a bit of a fool of himself on stage, the attraction between Gilles and Marion is clear to all three of them. Rather than go on the hike in the hills with Valérie they had planned, Gilles has sought Marion out on the beach, which thereby becomes a site of transition for both of them – from one relationship to another for him, and from the single status she has had for four months to 'attached' for her. The beach of *5 x 2* figures fluidity and undecidability in another way too, though since in the version of the film released in cinemas, the start of the couple's relationship is the last of the five episodes we see, but the DVD also offers a re-edited version in which the episodes play in chronological order. The beach is the beginning but also the end: it indicates an end and a beginning for Gilles and Marion, and holds a similar double status for the film-text of *5 x 2*. As such, it is a figure of undecidability that echoes (if it does not exactly overlap with) the significance the beach has as a ludic space, a place of experimental pleasure, in *Une robe d'été* and *Regarde la mer*.

Dirty and clean: the threat of the other

As might be expected of dramas about shifts in identity and sexual orientation, Ozon's films highlight oppositions of all kinds. One of

the most prominent recurring binary oppositions is between cleanliness, associated with states of safety and stability, and dirt, which
is linked to conditions of danger and infection. Tatiana, the *routarde*
who enters the life of Sasha and her baby in *Regarde la mer*, stands
out in the washed-clean setting of Sasha's husband's seaside cottage
because of her dark, dirty, ragged clothes, which she never seems
to remove – wearing them even on the beach with the baby, when
Sasha is sunbathing in a bikini. The grubbiness of Tatiana's body is
highlighted in a shot of just her lower legs when she is sitting on the
toilet, her very off-white pants around her ankles, with the bruises
and blemishes acquired from a routine of hiking and camping
clearly visible. More striking still is a shot of the contents of the toilet
basin, sticky brown faeces that Tatiana has not flushed away and that
contrast starkly with the bathroom's shining white enamel, as with
the overwhelming cleanness of most of the film's exteriors.[12] The
vagabond's dirtiness, along with her inexpressive demeanour and
taciturn manner, signal the danger Sasha fails to suspect for far too
long, a danger stemming from Tatiana's sense of the damage inflicted
on her during the birth of her baby, now dead. How her body has
been torn and wounded is a story too traumatic for her to tell in the
first person, but she reveals it in the scene where she suddenly asks
Sasha a barrage of questions about her toddler's birth (did she have
an epidural, did she need an episiotomy?), adding that she has heard
that childbirth tears some women right from the vagina to the anus.
Tatiana cannot have any more children, as childbirth has injured her
so badly that her reproductive organs have been contaminated by the
colon and its dirty, foul-smelling contents. This sense of damage and
loss resulting from her injury is what drives her to murder Sasha and
to kidnap her baby at the close of *Regarde la mer*, an act surprising in
its suddenness and its violence.

   An earlier short film from 1994, *Action vérité* (*Truth or Dare*), figures
the body's danger in a more innocent context. Ozon's world of pairs
and couples finds an obvious expression in this film's eponymous
game, played here by four adolescents (two of each gender), since
'Truth or Dare' is all about self-revelation, same-sex and cross-sex

12 'The cutting cleanness (precision) of *See the sea* is what strikes the viewer
   first. The framing is decided and decisive. The shots follow one another with
   diabolical precision, with an unfaltering sense of rhythm, impressively assured'
   (Jousse 1997: 66–7).

play, and infringing on the other's space or privacy – crossing over into his/her bodily territory. Examples of the challenges Paul, Rémy, Rose and Hélène trade range from the minor (licking a foot) to the audacious (Rose putting her hand into Hélène's knickers to tell what the smell is), but the game stops abruptly when, as she performs this dare, Rose finds menstrual blood – Hélène's first, it is clear from the expressions on all four faces – on her fingers. The social ritual of experimenting with sexual activity has inadvertently coincided with a personal rite of passage, transforming a discovery that is almost always private into one that is public, and rendering visible a taboo substance. Light-hearted yet charged adolescent play is stopped in its tracks as cognisance is taken of one of the most potent signs of the transition to adulthood and its responsibilities.

Cleanliness and dirt are also central to a third of Ozon's short films, X2000 (1998), which takes place the morning after a party to celebrate the new millennium. A post-party atmosphere is palpable in the apartment belonging to an unnamed couple, the man of which gets out of bed first to wander around the silent rooms. Distracted by the sight of a couple making love in the window of a flat opposite, several floors below (the setting of X2000 is Seine Saint-Denis, the outskirts of Paris, with its huge unadorned *grands ensembles* (municipal council housing)), he peers at them with such intent voyeurism that he falls off the window ledge on which he has been balancing, and breaks the glass that contained his effervescent hangover-remedy. In the meantime, his female partner, having spotted her lover's interest in another couple's physical passion and allowed a pained grimace to cross her face, unseen by him, has been relaxing in a warm bath, submerging every part of her body except her face. The man takes the shards of his broken glass to the kitchen bin, and discovers a small swarm of ants underneath and around it. Seeing the perturbation on his face as he crosses into the bathroom, the woman asks what the matter is, to which he replies simply 'Les fourmis attaquent!'.[13] A close-up of a few of them on his foot follows as if to confirm this rather melodramatic diagnosis. His gloom and concern relates superficially to the ants, whose appearance on the first morning of the new millennium works more obviously in a symbolic register, expressive of the decline of passion in the couple's relationship and

13 'The ants are attacking!'

the difficulties it may face in the future. They are both naked in every shot of *X2000*, but passion is seen only in the flat opposite, while the absence of it between the couple in their apartment is highlighted by the mesmerising image of communion formed by two twin brothers sharing a sleeping bag on the apartment's floor.

In *Regarde la mer*, *Action vérité* and *X2000*, dirt, vermin and abjected body contents (faeces and menstrual blood) signal danger, decline and fear or disgust in those who view them. *Sitcom* is alone among Ozon's films in presenting the ambiguity of such forms of life, manifested in the small white laboratory rat brought home by the family's father at the start of the film. While he, his son Nicolas and daughter Sophie are charmed by the rat, his wife is dismayed, but tolerates it because of her husband's calmly authoritarian hold over family life. Nicolas's enthralment to the rat's ambiguous appeal (it is vermin but clean, and although cute-looking, sometimes bites), is revealed when he is called to the dinner table by his mother just after the rat's arrival, and, rather than wetting his hands, carefully directs the flow of water from the tap between his fingers, giving the appearance of obeying her request to wash his hands rather than actually doing so. Nicolas's announcement that he is gay follows directly upon his captivation by the rat's charm, while not long afterwards, later that same evening, Sophie releases the rat from its cage and allows it to crawl all over her body, evidently experiencing sexualised pleasure from the contact: the rat's appeal is uncertain but clearly connected to sexuality.

Dark genres, lightness of touch

By discussing the evident importance to Ozon's cinema of unclean bodies, vermin and dirt generally, I have turned attention to his unarguable interest in death (including its connection with sex and sexuality) – what might in everyday parlance be termed the 'darkness' of his cinema. While some critics have sought to complain about this inclination to be psychological and dig into the 'ugly underbelly' of human relations,[14] a greater number have pursued the issue more

14 Charles Mudede objects to being reminded 'that violence, anger, cruelty and death all structure the moment of intercourse' (Mudede 2000: 2–3), and freely admits that although he thinks Ozon is talented, he finds him frustrating 'because he is psychological' (Mudede 2000: 3). Ozon 'should get out of the

fruitfully, via the issue of genre. The same moments and motifs I considered in the previous section of this chapter contribute to the several genres in which many of his films – particularly *Regarde la mer*, *Sitcom*, *Les Amants criminels*, *8 Femmes* and *Swimming Pool* – participate, without ever approximating to formulaic Hollywood-style 'genre cinema'. While *Sitcom* and *8 Femmes* undoubtedly owe some kind of debt to anti-bourgeois farce, neither film fits neatly inside the boundaries of a single genre: as Schilt observes, *8 Femmes* 'is a comedy, a melodrama and a whodunit, seasoned with a pinch of the musical' (Schilt 2004: 4). Two other films with musical interludes are *Une robe d'été*, where Sheila's 'Bang bang' makes the film's narrative possible by temporarily coming between the two male lovers, and *Gouttes d'eau sur pierres brûlantes*, where a dance by all four actors to a Tony Holliday song relieves events that are taking a decidedly tragic turn with a couple of minutes of highly entertaining camp levity.

A non-cinematic genre that marks both *Sitcom* and *Les Amants criminels* is the fairy tale. Animals often take on human form in fairy tales, and in *Sitcom*, the rat and the father of the family become indistinguishable after he cooks and consumes it. After this, the rat's symbolic role in the family's fortunes moves from a realistic register into something like pantomime as the father transmogrifies into a human-sized ferocious version of the pet. In *Les Amants criminels* there are multiple allusions to fairy tale, explicit among which is the woodsman's identity as an ogre (Alice whispers 'C'est un ogre!'[15] to Luc when they are first imprisoned in the woodsman's cellar). Earlier on, when the pair first venture into the woods, they mark their trail exactly as Hansel and Gretel do in the Grimm brothers' story, in order to be able to retrace it later – although since the woodsman tracks them as they do so, fairy-tale good fortune is thwarted. Returning to cinematic genres, the first part of *Les Amants criminels* bears more than a passing resemblance to a sequence of 'violent lovers on the run' films that goes back at least as far in film history as *Bonnie and Clyde* (1967), and was particularly successful in the 1990s, with Tony Scott's *True Romance* (1993) and Oliver Stone's *Natural Born Killers* (1994).

Broader generic modes in which *Regarde la mer* and *Swimming Pool* are respectively caught up are horror and the thriller. Many of Ozon's

---

cave of the mind, with its blood on the walls and bones on the ground, and ... just enjoy the sun' (Mudede 2000: 3).

15 'He's an ogre!'

reviewers comment on the precision and care with which suspense is built in *Regarde la mer*, where the final revelation that Tatiana is a psychopath still has the power to shock. In *Swimming Pool*, however, Ozon nails his generic colours to the mast straightaway, by making his chief character Sarah Morton (Charlotte Rampling's second role for Ozon following the critical and commercial success the duo found with *Sous le sable*) a writer of detective fiction – an obvious homage to women authors such as Patricia Highsmith, P. D. James and Patricia Cornwall. Ozon is on record as identifying closely with the character of Morton (Schilt 2004: 7), and in the same set of remarks, reveals that reflexive commentary on genre is part of *Swimming Pool*'s fabric ('*Swimming Pool* reflects my personal obsessions about creating, and ... it's a film about inspiration' (Schilt 2004: 7)). Finally in the catalogue of genres Ozon manipulates, there is melodrama, which as Fiona Handyside has argued of *Gouttes d'eau sur pierres brûlantes*, it is tempting to label 'metageneric': 'a reflexive performance of the role of genre in cinema' (Handyside 2005: 7). Whether or not Ozon's focus on domesticity and the family renders his cinema essentially melodramatic (this seems to be Handyside's view, whereas I prefer to emphasise the queer politics of Ozon's families, more important for the French context in which the films are made), it is certainly true that Ozon's 'use of genre asserts European cinema as a popular cinema, even as the languages ... and formalist occupations of the films would seem to label them as European art-cinema' (Handyside 2005: 1).

Ozon's ability to make entirely accessible and emotionally rich films while simultaneously working at a metacinematic level – on genre in *Gouttes d'eau* and *Swimming Pool*, on stardom in *8 Femmes* – is evidence that any heavy-handedness or crudity perceived (Bonnaud 2001) is due to inadequate appreciation of his singular blend of weighty emotional and sexual material with formal subtlety. Camp and kitsch that lighten dense or tragic action are an integral part of this queer cinema, which includes astonishing moments of wit. One of the best of these occurs near the end of the least successful of his features critically and commercially, *Les Amants criminels*, as Alice and Luc, just freed from the 'ogre's' lair but about to be apprehended by the police, engage in intercourse on a rock by the river that runs through the forest. Intercut with the shots of Luc still trying in vain to prove heterosexual potency are several carefully framed shots of a bird of prey, a hare, a fox, a deer and a dove, which emphasise the creatures' innocent wonder, as if out of a Disney film about the natural world.[16] As they look upon the young lovers or are filmed in the foreground with the pair in the background, the startling contrast of these innocent, beautiful animals of the forest with the desperate, ill-matched young criminals is a moment of pure irony and camp artifice in which Ozon sets natural splendour against the entirely non-natural complexity of human sexuality. While unmistakably still sympathising with his characters, he is distracted by and unable to pass up the opportunity for a knowing formal device. It is this – Ozon's evenhanded attention to both the complexity and difficulty of human sexuality *and* the capacities of cinema – that constitutes the doubleness of which his career in film has been made, up to now.

Conclusion: Ozon the *auteur*

Whether or not Ozon's films up to *5 x 2* exhibit the kind of thematic coherence sometimes demanded of *auteur* status, there is little doubt that he has generally been received as an *auteur* (albeit tardily and grudgingly by critics such as Bonnaud), both in his native France and internationally. I have implicitly acknowledged this in parts of my discussion, perhaps particularly in 'Dirty and clean: the threat of the other', which resembles *auteur*-structuralist criticism of the late 1960s and early 1970s in the way it finds deep-seated binary oppositions underlying – and therefore arguably structuring – Ozon's narratives. But if Ozon's focus on human and usually family dramas, on the couple, and on sexual relations generally, can make it seem as if his cinema is simply continuing to mine the traditional *intimiste* seam of drama still relied upon by a substantial proportion of French cinematic production, there is nothing polite or hide-bound about Ozon's twist on this tradition, which he has taken into new, more interesting, and sometimes shocking territory – queer territory. Perhaps most significantly where Ozon as *auteur* is concerned, at least three of his features (*Sous le sable*, *8 Femmes*, *Swimming Pool*) have seen audience figures and generated an order of box-office revenue that rival French films considered 'popular' successes, thereby undoing the binary opposi-

16 I am grateful to Darren Waldron for putting the name 'Disney' to the particular
   ideological slant of these shots.

tion between '*auteur*' and 'popular' cinema. But even if Ozon's appeal has been broad, there is as yet no critical consensus about why his cinema is important or the kind of *auteur* he is. The claim I would make is that he is best understood as France's first mainstream queer filmmaker.

References

Asibong, Andrew (2005), 'Meat, murder, metamorphosis: the transformational ethics of François Ozon', *French Studies*, 59:2 (April 2005), 203–15.

Bersani, Leo and Dutoit, Ulysse (2004), *Forms of Being: Cinema, Aesthetics, Subjectivity*, London, British Film Institute.

Bingham, Adam (2003), 'Identity and love: the not-so discreet charm of François Ozon', at www.kinoeye.org/printer.php?path=03/13/bingham13. php, accessed 03/08/2004.

Bonnaud, Frédéric (2001), 'François Ozon: wannabe *auteur* makes good', *Film Comment*, 37:4 (July–August), 52–5.

Butler, Judith (1990), *Gender Trouble: Feminism and the Subversion of Identity*, New York and London, Routledge.

Dean, Tim (2003), 'Lacan and queer theory', in Jean-Michel Rabaté (ed.), *The Cambridge Companion to Lacan*, Cambridge, Cambridge University Press, pp. 238–52.

Handyside, Fiona (2005), 'Flow, not form: melodrama in François Ozon's *Gouttes d'eau sur pierres brûlantes/Water Drops on Burning Rocks* (2000)', unpublished paper given at the *Studies in French Cinema* annual conference, Institut français, London, 30 March.

Higuinen, Erwan (2000), 'Avoir un projet d'avance', *Cahiers du cinéma*, 544 (March), 39–41.

Jousse, Thierry (1997), 'Sans toit ni loi', *Cahiers du cinéma*, 519 (December), 66–7.

Lalanne, Jean-Marc (2002), 'Les actrices: *Huit Femmes* de François Ozon', *Cahiers du cinéma*, 565 (February), 82–3.

Mudede, Charles (2000), 'Out of the cave: the convoluted, lousy appeal of François Ozon', *the Stranger* 9:49 (August 24–30), at www.thestranger. com/2000–08–24/film3.html, accessed 14/04/2005.

Ozon, François (2002), 'Dangerous dames', interview by Jeremiah Kipp in *Filmmaker: The Magazine of Independent Film* (26 September), at www. filmmakermagazine.com/archives/online_features/dangerous_dames. php, accessed 01/06/2005.

Romney, Jonathan (1999), 'Sitcom', *Sight and Sound* (January), 56.

Schilt, Thibault (2004), 'François Ozon', at www.sensesofcinema.com/ content/directors/04/ozon.html, accessed 03/08/2004.

Conclusion

Kate Ince

By focusing on the issue of auteurism in the introduction to this book, I left unmentioned other parallels and intersections between the films of Assayas, Audiard, the Dardenne brothers, Haneke and Ozon. One is that the long-standing binary opposition between 'European' (for which read 'art-house') and genre cinema is thoroughly deconstructed in the work of these directors, who have proved themselves able to master generic conventions and manipulate them to their own ends, while still respecting the power of genre as a means of communicating with the audience. (The most notable films here are Assayas' *demonlover*, Audiard's *Sur mes lèvres*, Haneke's *Caché* and Ozon's *8 Femmes*.) Several of the directors are visibly interested in materiality and corporeality: for Assayas this is mediated by the prominence of action and bodily performance in the genres he borrows from and reworks, while Audiard's filmmaking has been internally infiltrated by corporeality, evident in the attention to bodily senses and signs compelled by Carla's deafness in *Sur mes lèvres* and in Romain Duris's brilliantly nervy performance in *De battre mon coeur s'est arrêté*. In a comparable fashion, the Dardenne brothers have brought their filmmaking closer and closer to their protagonists' bodies in a way that emphasises the continuous struggle for survival, the effort of material and physical existence.

The most striking common ground occupied by some of this group of directors, however, must be the attention to ethical and political concerns that so profoundly marks the cinema of the Dardenne brothers and Haneke, and is arguably present in the complex patternings of desire in Ozon's films. What is often described as the 'return'

to the political in French-language cinema – although I shall avoid
so qualifying it, for the same reasons that I avoided referring, in my
introduction, to the international resurfacing of auteurism as a critical
paradigm at the start of the 1990s as a 'return' to the *auteur* – has
in recent writings usually been attributed to the phenomenon of the
jeune cinéma français, the more or less urgent social concern demonstrated by the films of a large number of young French directors in
the 1990s and early 2000s, whose output itself constituted a higher
proportion than ever before of the 200 plus films produced in France
each year. But although Ozon is of an age to belong to this questionable 'movement', the Dardenne brothers and Haneke, like Assayas
and Audiard, were already middle-aged and becoming established
directors when the *jeune cinéma français* was first identified as French
cinema's prevailing force. Where the Dardenne brothers and Haneke
are concerned, it seems more important to insist on how an urgent
concern with ethical and political matters influences their creation of
stories and choice of settings, and how it has progressively moulded
the form of their films into different but comparably powerful political aesthetics – the Dardenne brothers' singular realism of 'being
with' their characters, and Haneke's integration of his interrogation of
the image into his narratives. In the cinema of Audiard, too, political
questions are essential to the referential world of the narrative in *Un
héros très discret*.

The Dardenne brothers' and Haneke's privileging of ethical and
political perspectives takes place against the backdrop of societies
quite unlike that looked upon by any previous generation of film
spectators. We live in a media-saturated age in which political
progress is visibly hampered by the increasing interdependence, and
yet differing degrees of autonomy, of nation-states on a global stage.
Western societies are increasingly marked by a loss of the collective
at the level of local communities and of the family, and by fragile
social bonds. At such a point in history it is surely to be applauded
that there are still filmmakers who want to give their audiences
work to do – by making them reflect on how the pressing social and
personal issues that preoccupy them every day are inextricable from
larger, over-arching political frameworks, simultaneously local and
global. Haneke has been much criticised by some for his 'sadistic'
desire to goad his spectators into reflection (and perhaps action), but
although the material effort involved in the renewed, non-voyeuristic,

ethical kind of looking he wishes to shock us into is considerable, and the process can be uncomfortable, this is surely outweighed by any concrete change for the better induced by such 'productive unease'.

Filmography

All films are in colour unless otherwise stated (b/w). The format of feature films is 35mm unless otherwise stated, but has been specified for short films.

ASSAYAS

Short films

Copyright (1979), 35mm, 10 mins
Rectangle – Deux chansons de Jacno (1980), 35mm, 8 mins
Laissé inachevé à Tokyo (1982), b/w, 35mm, 20 mins
Winston Tong en studio (1984), 35mm, 10 mins

Feature films

Désordre (*Disorder*) (1986), 91 mins

Production: Forum Productions International, Virgin France, Centre National de la Cinématographie, Sofinergie
Screenplay: Olivier Assayas
Direction: Olivier Assayas
Photography: Denis Lenoir
Editing: Luc Barnier
Artistic direction: François-Renaud Labarthe
Sound: Philippe Sénéchal
Music: Gabriel Yared
Cast: Wadeck Stanczak (Yvan), Ann-Gisel Glass (Anne), Lucas

Belvaux (Henri), Rémi Martin (Xavier), Corinne Dacla (Cora), Simon de la Brosse (Gabriel), Etienne Chicot (Albertini), Philippe Demarle (Marc), Juliette Mailhe (Cécile), Etienne Daho (Jean-François)

L'Enfant de l'hiver (Winter's Child) (1989), 95 mins

Production: Gémini Films, G.P.F.I. (France), Sofica Investimage
Screenplay: Olivier Assayas
Direction: Olivier Assayas
Photography: Denis Lenoir
Editing: Luc Barnier
Artistic direction: François-Renaud Labarthe
Sound: Olivier Schwob
Music: Jorge Arriagada
Cast: Clotilde de Bayser (Sabine), Michel Feller (Stéphane), Maria Matheron (Natalia), Jean-Philippe Ecoffey (Bruno), Nathalie Richard (Leni)

Paris s'éveille (Paris Awakens/Paris at Dawn) (1991), 95 mins

Production: Aréna Films (Paris), Erre Produzioni, Christian Bourgois Productions, Films A2, Canal +, Sofica Investimage
Screenplay: Olivier Assayas
Direction: Olivier Assayas
Photography: Denis Lenoir
Editing: Luc Barnier
Artistic direction: François-Renaud Labarthe
Sound: Jean-Claude Laureux
Music: John Cale
Cast: Judith Godrèche (Louise), Thomas Langmann (Adrien), Jean-Pierre Léaud (Clément), Martin Lamotte (Zablonsky), Ounie Lecomte (Agathe), Antoine Basler (Victor)

Une nouvelle vie (A New Life) (1993), 122 mins

Production: Aréna Films (Paris), La Sept Cinéma, Vega Films, RTSR (Radio Télévision Suisse Romande)
Screenplay: Olivier Assayas
Direction: Olivier Assayas
Photography: Denis Lenoir
Editing: Luc Barnier
Artistic direction: François-Renaud Labarthe

Sound: François Musy
Music: Pierre Lorrain
Cast: Sophie Aubry (Tina), Judith Godrèche (Lise), Bernard Giraudeau (Constantin), Christine Boisson (Laurence), Philippe Torreton (Fred), Bernard Verley (Ludovic), Nelly Borgeaud (Nadine), Antoine Basler (Kleber), Roger Dumas (Martin)

L'Eau froide (Cold Water) (1994), 90 mins

Production: IMA Films, La Sept Cinéma, SFP Cinéma, Sony Music Entertainment
Screenplay: Olivier Assayas
Direction: Olivier Assayas
Photography: Denis Lenoir
Editing: Luc Barnier
Artistic direction: Gilbert Gagneux
Sound: Hervé Chauvel
Music: Janis Joplin, Nico, Roxy Music, Leonard Cohen, Creedence Clearwater Revival, Bob Dylan, Alice Cooper, Uriah Heep, Donovan
Cast: Virginie Ledoyen (Christine), Cyprien Fouquet (Gilles), László Szabó (Gilles' father), Jean-Pierre Darroussin (Inspector), Dominique Faysse (Christine's mother), Ismaïl Mekki (Mourad), Jackie Berroyer (Christine's father), Jean-Christophe Bouvet (Teacher), Ilona Györi (Marie)

Irma Vep (1996), 99 mins

Production: Dacia Films, Canal +
Screenplay: Olivier Assayas
Direction: Olivier Assayas
Photography: Eric Gautier
Editing: Luc Barnier
Artistic direction: François-Renaud Labarthe
Sound: Philippe Richard
Music: Philippe Richard, Yann Richard, Ry Cooder, Serge Gainsbourg, Thurston Moore
Cast: Maggie Cheung (Maggie), Jean-Pierre Léaud (René Vidal), Nathalie Richard (Zoë), Nathalie Boutefeu (Laure), Lou Castel (José Murano), Bulle Ogier (Mireille), Antoine Basler (Journalist), Alex Descas (Desormeaux), Dominique Faysse (Maïte), Bernard Nissile (Markus), Arsinée Khanjian (American woman), Estelle Larrivaz (switchboard operator)

HHH, portrait de Hou Hsiao Hsien (HHH, a Portrait of Hou Hsiao Hsien) (1997), 91 mins

Production: AMIP, Arc Light Films, Chinese Public Television, Hsu Hsiao-Ming Film Co., Institut National de l'Audiovisuel (INA), La Sept Arte
Screenplay: Olivier Assayas
Direction: Olivier Assayas
Photography: Eric Gautier
Editing: Marie Lecoeur
Artistic direction: François-Renaud Labarthe
Sound: Du-Che Tu, William Flageollet
Music: Du-Che Tu
Cast: Hsiao Hsien Hou (Himself), Kuo-fu Chen, Tien-wen Chu, She Kao, Giang Lin, Du-Che Tu, Nien-Jen Wu

Fin août, début septembre (Late August, Early September) (1999), 112 mins

Production: Dacia Films, Cinéa, Canal +, Centre National de la Cinématographie, Sofinergie, SofyGram
Screenplay: Olivier Assayas
Direction: Olivier Assayas
Photography: Denis Lenoir
Editing: Luc Barnier
Artistic direction: François-Renaud Labarthe
Sound: William Flageollet
Music: Ali Farka Touré
Cast: Mathieu Amalric (Gabriel), Virginie Ledoyen (Anne), François Cluzet (Adrien), Jeanne Balibar (Jenny), Alex Descas (Jérémie), Arsinée Khanjian (Lucie), Nathalie Richard (Maryelle), Mia Hansen-Løve (Véra), Eric Elmosnino (Thomas), Olivier Cruveiller (Axel)

Les Destinées sentimentales (Les Destinées/Sentimental Destinies) (2000), 180 mins

Production: Aréna Films (Paris), TF1 Film Productions, CAB Productions, Canal +, Cofimage 11, Eurimages Conseil de l'Europe, Centre National de la Cinématographie
Screenplay: Olivier Assayas
Direction: Olivier Assayas
Photography: Eric Gautier

Editing: Luc Barnier
Artistic direction: Katia Wyszkop
Sound: Jean-Claude Laureaux, William Flageollet
Music: Guillaume Lekeu
Cast: Emmanuelle Béart (Pauline), Charles Berling (Jean), Isabelle Huppert (Nathalie), Olivier Perrier (Philippe), Dominique Reymond (Julie), André Marcon (Paul), Alexandra London (Louise), Julie Depardieu (Marcelle), Jean-Baptiste Malartre (Frédéric), Mia Hansen-Løve (Aline), Rémi Martin (Dahlias)

demonlover (2002), 129 mins

Production: Elizabeth Films, M6, Citizen Films, TPS Cinéma, Procirep, Groupe Datacine, Cofimage 13, Gimages 5
Screenplay: Olivier Assayas
Direction: Olivier Assayas
Photography: Denis Lenoir
Editing: Luc Barnier
Artistic direction: François-Renaud Labarthe
Sound: Olivier Goinard
Music: Sonic Youth
Cast: Connie Nielsen (Diane), Charles Berling (Hervé), Chloë Sevigny (Elise), Gina Gershon (Elaine), Jean-Baptiste Malartre (Henri-Pierre), Dominique Reymond (Karen)

Clean (2004), 110 mins

Production: Rectangle Productions, Leap Films, 1551264 Ontario Inc., Arte France Cinéma, Haystack Productions, Rhombus Media, Canal+, Centre National de la Cinématographie, Téléfilm Canada, UK Film Council
Screenplay: Olivier Assayas
Direction: Olivier Assayas
Photography: Eric Gautier
Editing: Luc Barnier
Artistic direction: François-Renaud Labarthe
Sound: Daniel Sobrino
Music: Brian Eno, David Roback, Tricky
Cast: Maggie Cheung (Emily), Nick Nolte (Albrecht), Jeanne Balibar (Irène), Don McKeller (Vernon), Martha Henry (Rosemary), Rémi Martin (Jean-Pierre), Béatrice Dalle (Elena), Tricky (himself), David Roback (himself)

AUDIARD

Feature films

Regarde les hommes tomber (*See How They Fall*) (1994) 90 mins

Production: Bloody Mary productions, Centre Européen Ciné-matographique Rhône-Alpes, France 3 Cinéma
Screenplay: Jacques Audiard, Alain Le Henry, Teri White (novel)
Camera: Gérard Stein
Editing: Juliette Welfling
Sound: François Waledisch, Monique Dartonne
Music: Alexandre Desplat
Cast: Jean-Louis Trintignant (Marx), Jean Yanne (Simon), Mathieu Kassovitz (Johnny), Bulle Ogier (Laurie), Christine Pascal (Sandrine), Yvon Back (Mickey)

Un héros très discret (*A Self Made Hero*) (1996) 107 mins

Production: Alicéléo, Cofimage 7, Lumière, Studio Images 2
Screenplay: Jacques Audiard, Alain Le Henry, Jean-François Deniau (novel)
Camera: Jean-Marc Fabre
Editing: Juliette Welfling
Sound: Jean-Pierre Duret, Nicola Naegelen
Music: Alexandre Desplat
Cast: Mathieu Kassovitz (Albert Dehousse), Anouk Grinberg (Servane), Sandrine Kiberlain (Yvette), Jean-Louis Trintignant (old Albert Dehousse), Bernard Bloch (Ernst), Danièle Lebrun (Madame Dehousse), François Chattot (Louvier)

Sur mes lèvres (*Read My Lips*) (2001) 118 mins

Production: Canal +, CNC, Ciné B, France 2 Cinéma, Pathé Image Production, Sédif Productions
Screenplay: Jacques Audiard, Tonino Benacquista
Camera: Mathieu Vadepied
Editing: Juliette Welfling
Sound: Marc-Antoine Beldent, Gaël Nicolas
Music: Alexandre Desplat
Cast: Vincent Cassel (Paul), Emmanuelle Devos (Carla), Olivia Bonamy (Annie), Olivier Gourmet (Marchand), Olivier Perrier (Masson),

Bernard Alane (Morel), Pierre Diot (Keller), David Saracino (Richard Carambo), Christophe Van de Velde (Louis Carambo)

De battre mon coeur s'est arrêté (*The Beat That My Heart Skipped*) (2005) 107 mins

Production: Why Not Productions, Sédif Productions, France 3 Cinéma, Cofimage 15, Canal +, Ciné cinemas
Screenplay: Jacques Audiard, Tonino Benacquista, James Toback (earlier screenplay)
Camera: Stéphane Fontaine
Editing: Juliette Welfling
Sound: Brigitte Taillandier, Nikolas Javelle
Music: Alexandre Desplat
Cast: Romain Duris (Thomas Seyr), Aure Atika (Aline), Niels Arestup (Robert Seyr), Lin Dan Pham (Miao Lin), Gilles Cohen (Sami), Jonathan Zaccaï (Fabrice), Emmanuelle Devos (Chris), Anton Yakovlev (Minskov)

DARDENNE BROTHERS

Short films

Lorsque le bateau de Léon M. descendit la Meuse pour la première fois (1979), video, 40 mins

Production: Collectif Dérives
Direction: Jean-Pierre and Luc Dardenne
Camera: Jean-Pierre Dardenne
Sound: Luc Dardenne

Pour que la guerre s'achève les murs devaient s'écrouler (Le Journal) (1980), video, 50 mins

Production: RTBF (Vidéographie), Collectif Dérives, Fleur Maigre Coop.
Direction: Jean-Pierre and Luc Dardenne
Camera: Lucien Ronday
Sound: Robert Joris
Montage: Francis Galopin

Regarde Jonathan. Jean Louvet, son oeuvre (1983), video, 57 mins

Production: Dérives, Wallonie Image Production, Notélé Tournai, RTBF (Charleroi)
Direction: Jean-Pierre and Luc Dardenne
Camera: Claude Mouriéras
Sound: Jean-Pierre Duret and Dominique Warnier
Montage: Guy Souphy and Jean-Pierre and Luc Dardenne
Production design and costumes: Jean-Claude de Bemels

Feature films

Je pense à vous (1992), 93 mins

Production: Films Dérives, Favourite Films, Titane, Samsa Film, RTBF (Télévision belge), Le Centre Bruxellois de l'Audiovisuel (CBA)
Direction: Jean-Pierre and Luc Dardenne
Screenplay: Jean Gruault, Jean-Pierre and Luc Dardenne
Cinematography: Yorgos Arvanitis
Sound: Jean-Pierre Duret
Editing: Ludo Troch, Denise Vindevogel
Production design: Yves Brover-Rabinovici
Costume Design: Monic Parelle
Cast: Robin Renucci (Fabrice), Fabienne Babe (Céline), Tolsty (Marek), Gil Lagay (Renzo), Pietro Pizzuti (Laurent)

La Promesse (1996), 90 mins

Production: Les Films du fleuve, Touza Productions, Samsa Film, RTBF (Télévision belge)
Direction: Jean-Pierre and Luc Dardenne
Screenplay: Jean-Pierre and Luc Dardenne, Léon Michaux, Alphonse Badolo
Cinematography: Alain Marcoen
Camera: Benoît Dervaux
Sound: Jean-Pierre Duret
Editing: Marie-Hélène Dozo
Production design: Igor Gabriel
Costume Design: Monic Parelle
Cast: Jérémie Renier (Igor), Olivier Gourmet (Roger), Assita Ouédraogo (Assita), Frédéric Bodson (Garage boss), Rasmané Ouédraogo (Amidou)

Rosetta (1999), 90 mins

Production: Les Films du fleuve, RTBF (Télévision belge), ARP Sélection
Direction: Jean-Pierre and Luc Dardenne
Screenplay: Jean-Pierre and Luc Dardenne
Cinematography: Alain Marcoen
Camera: Benoît Dervaux
Sound: Jean-Pierre Duret
Editing: Marie-Hélène Dozo
Production design: Igor Gabriel
Costume Design: Monic Parelle
Cast: Émilie Dequenne (Rosetta), Fabrizio Rongione (Riquet), Anne Yernaux (Rosetta's mother), Olivier Gourmet (the boss), Bernard Marbaix (the campsite manager)

Le Fils (*The Son*) (2002), 103 mins

Production: Les Films du fleuve, Archipel 35, RTBF (Télévision belge)
Direction: Jean-Pierre and Luc Dardenne
Screenplay: Jean-Pierre and Luc Dardenne
Cinematography: Alain Marcoen
Camera: Benoît Dervaux
Sound: Jean-Pierre Duret
Editing: Marie-Hélène Dozo
Production design: Igor Gabriel
Costume design: Monic Parelle
Cast: Olivier Gourmet (Olivier), Morgan Marinne (Francis), Isabella Soupart (Magali)

L'Enfant (*The Child*) (2005), 91 mins

Production: Les Films du Fleuve, Archipel 35, RTBF (Télévision belge), Scope Invest, Arte France Cinéma
Direction: Jean-Pierre and Luc Dardenne
Screenplay: Jean-Pierre and Luc Dardenne
Cinematography: Alain Marcoen
Camera: Benoît Dervaux
Sound: Jean-Pierre Duret
Editing: Marie-Hélène Dozo
Production design: Igor Gabriel

Costume design: Monic Parelle
Cast: Jérémie Renier (Bruno), Déborah François (Sonia), Jérémie Ségard (Steve), Fabrizio Rongione (young crook), Frédéric Bodson (older crook), Mireille Bailly (Bruno's mother), Stéphane Bissot (woman fence)

HANEKE

Feature films

Der siebente Kontinent (*The Seventh Continent*) (1989), 90 mins

Production: Wega Film
Screenplay: Michael Haneke
Photography: Anton Peschke
Editing: Marie Homolkova
Artistic direction: Rudolf Czettel
Sound: Karl Schlifelner
Cast: Dieter Berner (Georg), Birgit Doll (Anna), Leni Tanzer (Eva), Udo Samel (Alexander)

Benny's Video (1992), 105 mins

Production: Wega Film
Screenplay: Michael Haneke
Photography: Christian Berger
Editing: Marie Homolkova
Artistic direction: Christoph Kanter
Sound: Karl Schlifelner
Cast: Arno Frisch (Benny), Angela Winkler (mother), Ulrich Mühe (father), Ingrid Stassner (girl)

71 Fragmente einer Chronologie des Zufalls (*71 Fragments of a Chronology of Chance*) (1994), 96 mins

Production: Wega Film
Screenplay: Michael Haneke
Photography: Christian Berger
Editing: Marie Homolkova
Artistic direction: Christoph Kanter
Sound: Marc Parisotto

Cast: Gabriel Cosmin Urdes (Marian Radu), Lukas Miko (Max), Otto Grünmandl (Tomek), Anne Bennent (Inge Brunner), Udo Samel (Paul Brunner), Branko Samarovski (Hans), Claudia Martini (Maria), Georg Friedrich (Bernie)

Funny Games (1997), 108 mins

Production: Wega Film
Screenplay: Michael Haneke
Photography: Jürgen Jürges
Editing: Andreas Prochaska
Artistic direction: Christoph Kanter
Sound: Walter Amann, Bernhard Bamberger, Hannes Eder
Cast: Susanne Lothar (Anna), Ulrich Mühe (Georg), Arno Frisch (Paul), Frank Giering (Peter), Stefan Clapczynski (Schorschi)

Code inconnu: récit incomplet de divers voyages (*Code Unknown*) (2000), 118 mins

Production: MK2 Productions, Les Films Alain Sarde, Bavaria Film, Filmex Romania, France 2 Cinéma, Arte France Cinéma
Screenplay: Michael Haneke
Photography: Jürgen Jürges
Editing: Karin Martusch, Nadine Muse, Andreas Prochaska
Artistic direction: Emmanuel de Chauvigny
Sound: Eric Ferret, Jean-Pierre Laforce, Nadine Muse, Guillaume Sciama
Music: Giba Gonçalves
Cast: Juliette Binoche (Anne Laurent), Thierry Neuvic (Georges), Josef Bierbichler (farmer), Alexandre Hamidi (Jean), Ona Lu Yenke (Amadou), Luminita Gheorghiu (Maria), Maimouna Hélène Diarra (Aminate), Djibril Kouyaté (Youssouf)

La Pianiste (*The Piano Teacher*) (2001), 131 mins

Production: Wega Film, MK2 Productions, Les Films Alain Sarde, Arte France Cinéma
Screenplay: Michael Haneke (adapted from the novel by Elfriede Jelinek)
Photography: Christian Berger
Editing: Nadine Muse, Monika Willi
Artistic direction: Christoph Kanter
Sound: Jean-Pierre Laforce, Nadine Muse, Guillaume Sciama

Music: Francis Haines
Cast: Isabelle Huppert (Erika Kohut), Annie Girardot (mother), Benoît Magimel (Walter Klemmer), Anna Sigalevitch (Anna Schober), Susanne Lothar (Frau Schober)

Le Temps du loup (The Time of the Wolf) (2003), 110 mins

Production: Bavaria Film, Les Films du Losange, Wega Film
Screenplay: Michael Haneke
Photography: Jürgen Jürges
Editing: Nadine Muse, Monika Willi
Artistic direction: Christoph Kanter, James David Goldmark
Sound: Jean-Pierre Laforce, Guillaume Sciama
Cast: Isabelle Huppert (Anne Laurent), Anaïs Demoustier (Eva), Lucas Biscombe (Ben), Hakim Taleb (runaway), Béatrice Dalle (Lise Brandt), Patrice Chéreau (Thomas Brandt), Rona Hartner (Arina), Maurice Bénichou (M. Azoulay), Olivier Gourmet (Koslowski), Brigitte Roüan (Béa), Serge Riaboukine (leader), Daniel Duval (Georges Laurent)

Caché (Hidden) (2005), 117 mins

Production: Les Films du Losange, Wega Film, Bavaria Film, BIM Distribuzione
Screenplay: Michael Haneke
Photography: Christian Berger
Editing: Michael Hudecek, Nadine Muse
Artistic direction: Emmanuel de Chauvigny, Christoph Kanter
Sound: Jean-Paul Mugel, Jean-Pierre Laforce
Music: Ralph Rieckermann
Cast: Daniel Auteuil (Georges Laurent), Juliette Binoche (Anne Laurent), Maurice Bénichou (Majid), Annie Girardot (Georges's mother), Walid Afkir (Majid's son), Lester Makedonsky (Pierrot Laurent), Daniel Duval (Pierre), Nathalie Richard (Mathilde), Denis Podalydès (Yvon), Aïssa Maïga (Chantal), Bernard Le Coq (chief editor)

Collaborative films

Lumière et compagnie (Lumière and Company) (1995), b/w and col, 92 mins

Production: Cinétévé, La Sept-Arte, Igeldo Komunikazioa, Søren Stærmose AB, Musée du Cinéma de Lyon
Direction: Merzak Allouache, Theo Angelopoulos, Vicente Aranda,

Gabriel Axel, J.J. Bigas Luna, John Boorman, Youssef Chahine, Alain Corneau, Constantin Costa-Gavras, Raymond Depardon, Francis Girod, Peter Greenaway, Lasse Hallström, Michael Haneke, Hugh Hudson, James Ivory, Gaston Kabore, Abbas Kiarostami, Cédric Klapisch, Andrei Konchalovsky, Patrice Leconte, Spike Lee, Claude Lelouch, David Lynch, Ismail Merchant, Claude Miller, Sarah Moon, Idrissa Ouédraogo, Arthur Penn, Lucian Pintilie, Jacques Rivette, Helma Sanders-Brahms, Jerry Schatzberg, Nadine Trintignant, Fernando Trueba, Liv Ullman, Jaco van Dormael, Régis Wargnier, Wim Wenders, Yoshishige Yoshida, Yimou Zhang

Operating the camera of the Lumière brothers: Didier Ferry, Philippe Poulet

Photography: Sarah Moon

Editing: Roger Ikhlef, Timothy Miller

Artistic direction: Anne Adreu

Sound: Jean Casanova, Cécile Lecante, Bernard Rochut

Music: Jean-Jacques Lemêtre

Television

Das Schloß (*The Castle*) (1997), 123 mins

Production: Bayerischer Rundfunk, Wega Film, Arte, Österreich-ischer Rundfunk

Screenplay: Michael Haneke (adapted from the novel by Franz Kafka)

Photography: Jirí Stibr

Editing: Andreas Prochaska

Artistic direction: Christoph Kanter

Cast: Ulrich Mühe (K), Susanne Lothar (Frieda), Frank Giering (Artur), Felix Eitner (Jeremias), André Eisermann (Barnabas), Johannes Silberschneider (teacher), Paulus Manker (Momus), Nikolaus Paryla (council chairman)

OZON

Short films

Photo de famille (*Family Photo*) (1988), Super-8, 7 mins

Cast: Guillaume Ozon (son), Anne-Marie Ozon (mother), René Ozon (father), Julie Ozon (daughter)

Victor (1993), 35mm, 14 mins

Cast: François Genty (Victor)

Action vérité (*Truth or Dare*) (1994), 35mm, 4 mins

Cast: Farida Rahmatoullah (Hélène), Aglin Argun (Rose), Fabien Billet (Rémy), Adrien Pastor (Paul)

La Petite Mort (*Little Death*)(1995), 35mm, 26 mins

Cast: François Delaive (Paul), Camille Japy (Camille), Jacques Martial (Martial), Michel Beaujard (the father)

Jospin s'éclaire (1995), 35mm, 54 mins, documentary of Lionel Jospin's 1995 presidential campaign

Une robe d'été (*A Summer Dress*) (1996), 35mm, 15 mins

Cast: Sébastien Charles (Sébastien), Lucia Sanchez (Lucia), Frédéric Mangenot (Luc)

Regarde la mer (*See the Sea*) (1997), 35mm, 52 mins

Cast: Sasha Hails (Sasha), Marina de Van (Tatiana)

Scènes de lit (*Bed Scenes*) (1998), 35mm, 26 mins

Cast: Valérie Druguet (prostitute), François Delaive (client), Camille Japy (woman in *M. Propre*), Philippe Dajoux (M. Propre in *M. Propre*), Evelyne Ker (woman in *Madame*), Loïc Even (youth in *Madame*), Lucia Sanchez (woman in *Tête bêche*), François Genty (man in *Tête bêche*), Pascale Arbillot (blonde in *L'Homme idéal*), Régine Mondion (blonde's friend in *L'Homme idéal*), Margot Abascal (Virginie), Bruno Slagmulder (Frank), Sébastien Charles (gay lover in *Les Puceaux*), Jérémie Elkaim (Paul)

X2000 (1998), 35mm, 6 mins

Cast: Denise Aron-Schropfer (the woman), Bruno Slagmulder (the man)

Feature films

Sitcom (1998), 80 mins

Production: Fidelité Productions
Screenplay: François Ozon
Cinematography: Yorick Le Saux
Editing: Dominique Petrot
Production design: Angélique Puron
Costume design: Hervé Poeydemenge
Music: Eric Neveux
Sound: François Guillaume
Cast: Evelyne Dandry (the mother), François Marthouret (the father), Marina de Van (Sophie), Adrien de Van (Nicolas), Stéphane Rideau (David), Lucia Sanchez (Maria), Jules-Emmanuel Eyoum Deido (Abdu)

Les Amants criminels (Criminal Lovers) (1998), 90 mins

Production: Canal+, Centre National de Cinématographie, Fidelité Productions, La Sept Cinéma
Writing credits: François Ozon (screenplay, dialogue, poem), Marina de Van (poem), Annabelle Perrichon and Marcia Romano (screenplay)
Cinematography: Pierre Stoeber
Editing: Claudine Bouché, Dominique Petrot
Art direction: Arnaud de Moleron
Set decoration: Pierre Griffon, Marc Thiébault
Costume design: Pascaline Chavanne
Sound: Benoît Hillebrant
Cast: Natacha Régnier (Alice), Jérémie Renier (Luc), Miki Manojlovic (the woodsman)

Gouttes d'eau sur pierres brûlantes (Water Drops on Burning Rocks) (1999), 90 mins

Production: Euro Space Inc, Fidelité Productions, Les Films Alain Sarde, Studio Images 6

Writing credits: Rainer Werner Fassbinder (play), François Ozon (screenplay)
Cinematography: Jeanne Lapoirie
Editing: Laurence Bawedin, Claudine Bouché
Production design: Arnaud de Moleron
Set decoration: Valérie Chemain
Costume design: Pascaline Chavanne
Sound: Benoît Hillebrant
Cast: Bernard Giraudeau (Léopold), Malik Zidi (Franz), Ludivine Sagnier (Anna), Anna Levine (Véra)

Sous le sable (*Under the Sand*) (2000), 95 mins

Production: Euro Space, Fidelité Productions, Haut et Court, Arte France Cinéma
Writing credits: Emmanuèle Bernheim, François Ozon, Marina de Van, Marcia Romano
Cinematography: Antoine Héberlé, Jeanne Lapoirie
Editing: Laurence Bawedin
Production design and Art direction: Sandrine Canaux
Costume design: Pascaline Chavanne
Sound: Benoît Hillebrant
Music: Philippe Rombi
Cast: Charlotte Rampling (Marie), Bruno Cremer (Jean)

8 Femmes (*8 Women*) (2001), 103 mins

Production: BIM, Canal+, Centre National de Cinématographie, Fidelité Productions, France 2 Cinéma, Gimages 5, Local Films, Mars Films
Writing credits: Robert Thomas (play), François Ozon and Marina de Van (screenplay)
Cinematography: Jeanne Lapoirie
Editing: Laurence Bawedin
Production design: Arnaud de Moleron
Set decoration: Marie-Claire Quin
Costume Design: Pascaline Chavanne
Art direction: Mick Lanaro (music art director)
Music: Krishna Levy
Sound: Benoît Hillebrant
Cast: Danielle Darrieux (Mamy), Catherine Deneuve (Gaby), Isabelle

Huppert (Augustine), Emmanuelle Béart (Louise), Fanny Ardant (Pierrette), Virginie Ledoyen (Suzon), Ludivine Sagnier (Catherine), Firmine Richard (Madame Chanel)

Swimming Pool (2003), 102 mins

Production: Fidelité Productions, France 2 Cinéma, Gimages, Foz
Writing credits: François Ozon (screenplay), Emmanuèle Bernheim, Sionann O'Neill (translation into English)
Cinematography: Yorick Le Saux
Editing: Monica Coleman
Art direction: Wouter Zoon
Set decoration: Brice Blasquez
Costume design: Pascaline Chavanne
Music: Philippe Rombi
Sound: Benoît Hillebrant
Cast: Charlotte Rampling (Sarah Morton), Ludivine Sagnier (Julie), Charles Dance (John Bosload)

5 x 2 (2004), 90 mins

Production: Canal+, Foz, Fidelité Productions, France 2 Cinéma
Screenplay: François Ozon, Emmanuèle Bernheim (collaborator)
Cinematography: Yorick Le Saux
Editing: Monica Coleman
Production design: Katia Wyszkup
Set decoration: Sophie Martel
Costume Design: Pascaline Chavanne
Music: Philippe Rombi, Ennio Morricone
Sound: Jean-Pierre Duvet, Brigitte Taillandier
Cast: Valéria Bruni-Tedeschi (Marion), Stéphane Freiss (Gilles)

Index